Games for Language Learning

Third Edition

Cambridge Handbooks for Language Teachers

This series, now with over 40 titles, offers practical ideas, techniques and activities for the teaching of English and other languages providing inspiration for both teachers and trainers.

Recent titles in this series:

Learner Autonomy
A guide to developing learner responsibility
ÁGOTA SCHARLE *and* ANITA SZABÓ

Personalizing Language Learning
GRIFF GRIFFITHS *and* KATHRYN KEOHANE

Teaching Adult Second Language Learners
HEATHER MCKAY *and* ABIGAIL TOM

Teaching Business English
SYLVIE DONNA

Teaching English Spelling
A practical guide
RUTH SHEMESH *and* SHEILA WALLER

Using Folktales
ERIC K. TAYLOR

Learner English (Second Edition)
A teacher's guide to interference and other problems
edited by MICHAEL SWAN *and* BERNARD SMITH

Planning Lessons and Courses
Designing sequences of work for the language classroom
TESSA WOODWARD

Teaching Large Multilevel Classes
NATALIE HESS

Using the Board in the Language Classroom
JEANNINE DOBBS

Laughing Matters
Humour in the language classroom
PÉTER MEDGYES

Stories
Narrative activities in the language classroom
RUTH WAJNRYB

Using Authentic Video in the Language Classroom
JANE SHERMAN

Extensive Reading Activities for Teaching Language
edited by JULIAN BAMFORD *and* RICHARD R. DAY

Language Activities for Teenagers
edited by SETH LINDSTROMBERG

Pronunciation Practice Activities
A resource book for teaching English pronunciation
MARTIN HEWINGS

Drama Techniques (Third Edition)
A resource book of communication activities for language teachers
ALAN MALEY *and* ALAN DUFF

Five-Minute Activities for Business English
PAUL EMMERSON *and* NICK HAMILTON

Dictionary Activities
CINDY LEANEY

Dialogue Activities
Exploring spoken interaction in the language class
NICK BILBROUGH

Five-Minute Activities for Young Learners
PENNY MCKAY *and* JENNI GUSE

The Internet and the Language Classroom (Second Edition)
A practical guide for teachers
GAVIN DUDENEY

Working with Images
A resource book for the language classroom
BEN GOLDSTEIN

Grammar Practice Activities (Second Edition)
A practical guide for teachers
PENNY UR

Games for Language Learning

THIRD EDITION

Andrew Wright
David Betteridge
Michael Buckby

CAMBRIDGE
UNIVERSITY PRESS

CAMBRIDGE UNIVERSITY PRESS
Cambridge, New York, Melbourne, Madrid, Cape Town,
Singapore, São Paulo, Delhi, Mexico City

Cambridge University Press
The Edinburgh Building, Cambridge CB2 8RU, UK

www.cambridge.org
Information on this title: www.cambridge.org/9780521618229

First published 1979
Second edition 1984
Third edition 2006
10th printing 2012

Printed and bound in the United Kingdom by the MPG Books Group

A catalogue record for this publication is available from the British Library

Library of Congress in Cataloguing in Publication data
Wright, Andrew, 1937–
Games for language learning / Andrew Wright, David Betteridge,
Michael Buckby. – 3rd ed.
          p.   cm. – (Cambridge handbooks for language teachers)
Includes bibliographical references and index.
ISBN 978-0-521-61822-9
1. Languages, Modern – Study and teaching.   2. Educational games.
I. Betteridge, David.   II. Buckby, Michael.   III. Title.   IV. Series.
PB35.W7 2005
418.0071–dc22   2005032579

ISBN 978-0-521-61822-9 Paperback

Contents

Contents

Contents

Contents

Preface to the Third Edition

This book has enjoyed a relatively long life since its first publication in 1979, serving language teaching (and language learning) needs in a great variety of schools and colleges across the world. It has been translated into many languages. A revised and greatly enlarged second edition was published in 1984, and has proved very popular.

We have learned that many teachers of languages other than English have found the book to be useful. They have reported to us that the games are essentially engaging and that their language concerns can easily be substituted for English in many, though not all, cases.

Over the years, we have gathered a great deal of information from teachers in many different countries concerning their experience of using our games with their students. In this third edition we have drawn on this rich experience and made a number of changes accordingly. Here they are:

- The eight sections of the book are based on broad teaching aims, e.g. *Mainly speaking*, rather than on types of games, e.g. *Picture games*, as in earlier editions. However, the book continues to support those teachers who want to adapt our games or create new ones of their own. It does this through the idea of families of games, that is, games in which the learners Connect, or Discriminate, or Create, or whatever. Within each section the games are grouped according to family.
- Concern for the individual learner has come to the forefront of teaching in recent years, and we have tried to reflect this in the choice and presentation of games. We have included a new section, *Solo games*; and we have included games covering a wide spectrum of individual preferences in ways of learning (visual, auditory, kinaesthetic, etc.).
- The book has always been a basic handbook of games, but in this new edition we have tried to strengthen that claim. In particular we have tried to support the new teacher or teacher in training by offering a wide range of games which are easily adaptable to different classes and to different learner needs.

Our aim: If you can only take one book with you ... take this one!

Acknowledgements

We would like to acknowledge a debt to Donn Byrne, Paul Davis, June Derrick, Alan Duff, Josie Levine, Alan Maley, John Morgan, Mario Rinvolucri and Jim Wingate.

We would also like to thank the many other colleagues who have contributed such a richness of games and activities to the world of language teaching over the last twenty-five years, both in the classroom and through books, articles and talks at conferences. We have benefited from their insights and practicalities.

In working on the third edition of this book, we have especially benefited from the advice of Eva Benko, Klara Czirle, Julia Dudas and David A. Hill; and from the many helpful suggestions, based on a detailed reading of our draft manuscript, made by Carrie Loffree and Tom McCarthy.

Our editor at Cambridge University Press, Alyson Maskell, has been perfect. She has blended compassion for us as writers, concern for the practical needs of teachers, and professionalism in steering the successive drafts of the book to its present form.

In spite of all this wonderful help, any mistakes remain our responsibility.

Drawings by Andrew Wright

Introduction

The aims of this book: a summary
1 To provide a wide range of games.
2 To give examples which are suitable for all levels of proficiency, but with an emphasis on beginners to intermediate.
3 To minimise competition and maximise challenge, creation, play.
4 To minimise exposure to failure and maximise success for all learners.
5 To give examples of texts which are ready to use.
6 To help the teacher to use, adapt or invent games.

Who is the book for?

This collection of language games is mainly for learners from beginner to intermediate level, although many of the games can be adapted for use with advanced proficiency learners as well. The examples that are given are for learners of secondary school age and above, although teachers of younger children will be able to adapt many of the examples. We have tried to make the book of particular relevance to beginner teachers who would like to have a handbook of a wide selection of games. We also hope that more experienced teachers will find that the range of games (and variations of games) makes this a useful collection, which might inspire them to adapt or create games of their own.

What is a game?

For the purpose of all three editions of this book we have taken the word 'game' to mean an activity which is entertaining and engaging, often challenging, and an activity in which the learners play and usually interact with others. A testing question might be: 'Would the learners be happy to do this activity in their own language?' We would like all our games to pass this test. Competition against others is not an essential ingredient of games, but challenge often is. In selecting and describing our games we have tried to minimise competition, with winners and losers, and to maximise challenge, where everyone feels inspired to 'have a go' and do their best. Competition may be stimulating for some, but it can also be destructive, making players anxious, with losers categorising themselves as 'no good' and the winners categorising themselves as 'very good'. Neither of these things may be true, and neither helps learning.

Why games?

Language learning is hard work

Language learning is hard work. One must make an effort to understand, to repeat accurately, to adapt and to use newly understood language in conversation and in written composition. Effort is required at every moment and must be maintained over a long period of time. Games help and encourage many learners to sustain their interest and work.

Experiencing language

Games also help the teacher to create contexts in which the language is useful and meaningful. The learners want to take part, and in order to do so must understand what others are saying or have written, and they must speak or write in order to express their own point of view or give information. Games provide one way of helping the learners to *experience* language rather than merely *study* it.

Repeated use of language items

Many games cause as much use of particular language items as more conventional drill exercises; some games do not. What matters, however, is the quality of practice.

The contribution of drill exercises lies in the concentration on a language form and its frequent occurrence during a limited period of time. Many games similarly provide repeated occurrence and use of a particular language form. By making language convey information and opinion, games provide the key features of 'drill' with the added opportunity to sense the working of language as living communication. Games involve the emotions, and the meaning of the language is thus more vividly experienced. It is, for this reason, probably better absorbed than learning based on mechanical drills.

Central to learning

If it is accepted that games can provide intense and meaningful practice of language, then they must be regarded as *central* to a language teacher's repertoire and not merely a way of passing the time.

Class, individual, pair, and group work

Opportunity for every learner to use the language

Of the four types of grouping, individual, pair, and group work are of especial value in ensuring that each and every learner has optimum opportunity for oral practice in using language, going beyond what is possible in class work.

Pair work

Pair work is easy and fast to organise. It provides opportunities for intensive listening and speaking practice. Pair work is usually better than group work if there are discipline problems.

Group work

Some games *require* four to six players; in these cases group work is essential. If there is to be competition between groups, they should be of mixed ability. If there is to be no such challenge, the teacher might choose groups according to ability: this is very much a personal choice. Many teachers consider it advisable to have a group leader. However, it is our experience that groups can operate perfectly well without a group leader. The leader would normally be one of the more able learners. However, there is much to be said for encouraging a reticent learner by giving the responsibility to him or her. The leader's role is to ensure that the game is properly organised, and to act as an intermediary between learners and teacher.

What about mistakes?

The greatest 'mistake' (if oral ability is an aim) is for the learner not to speak at all! Thus, although some mistakes of grammar or pronunciation or idiom may be made in pair or group work, the price is worth paying. If the learners are clear about what they have to do and the language is not beyond them, there need be few mistakes.

The teacher's role

The teacher's role, once the groups or pairs are in action, is to go from group to group listening in, contributing and, *if necessary*, correcting.

   If you have not organised group work before, then it is advisable to work slowly towards it. First of all, make the learners familiar with work in pairs. Add to this games in which rows of learners (if that is how they are seated) play against you or between themselves. Finally, after perhaps several weeks, ask the rows of learners to group themselves together to play a game between themselves.

To minimise difficulties, it is essential that the learners are very familiar with the games they are asked to play. (It is helpful if they are familiar with the game in their own language.)

Once the learners are familiar with group work, new games are normally introduced in the following way:

1   explanation by the teacher to the class
2   demonstration of parts of the game by the teacher and one or two learners
3   trial by a group in front of the class
4   any key language and/or instructions written on the board
5   first 'try out' of the game, by groups
6   key language, etc., removed from the board
7   the game continues.

Types of game

Being aware of the essential character of a type of game (see below) and the way in which it engages the learner can be helpful in the adaptation of games or the creation of new games.

The games in this edition of the book are grouped according to their family type within each of the eight sections. The family name is always a verb. This verb summarises the most important way in which the learners are engaged in the game, for example, IDENTIFY or CREATE. In every case this verb refers to the mental engagement on the part of the learners. The use of language arises out of the way the learner is engaged.

CARE AND SHARE

'Caring and sharing' games include all those games in which the learner feels comfortable while sharing personal information with other learners. These games relate more to invitation than to challenge. The striving implied by challenge is incompatible with the notion of 'caring and sharing'. The origin of this established phrase is the title of the classic book written by Gertrude Moskowitz, *Caring and Sharing in the Foreign Language Class* (Newbury House 1978).

See games 1.1–1.12.

DO: *MOVE, MIME, DRAW, OBEY*

The learner is expected to do something non-verbally in response to a read or a heard text.

See, for example, games 3.1, 5.1, 7.1.

IDENTIFY: *DISCRIMINATE, GUESS, SPECULATE*

The learner is challenged to identify something which is difficult to identify or to hypothesise about something which is then compared with the facts.

See, for example, games 2.1, 5.2, 7.4.

DESCRIBE

The learner is challenged to describe something to another learner, by speaking or writing, so well that the other learner can do something, for example, draw a picture. The learner may describe something objectively or subjectively, communicating his or her own feelings and associations.

See, for example, games 2.3, 4.2, 7.15.

CONNECT: *COMPARE, MATCH, GROUP*

The learner is challenged to connect, compare, match or group various items of information, perhaps pictures or texts, objectively or subjectively. He or she uses language to describe or comment on the pairs or groups of information.

See, for example, games 3.6, 6.7, 7.16.

ORDER

The learner is challenged to put various bits of information into an order of quality and importance, subjectively or objectively, or to put texts, pictures, objects, into a developmental sequence, also subjectively or objectively.

See, for example, games 5.6, 6.10, 7.18.

REMEMBER

The learner tries to remember something and then communicate what he or she has remembered.

See, for example, games 5.8, 6.11, 7.21.

CREATE

The learner is challenged or invited to make a story, write a poem or produce some other kind of material using their imagination. Here the distinction between 'challenged' and 'invited' is worth making. 'Challenged' might include those story-making starters in which you stipulate certain features: for example, you stipulate that a certain tense form must occur very often, or that the story must be exactly 50 words long. 'Invited', because sometimes the best way to stir the creative forces is to 'invite', 'encourage', 'show interest', and so on.

See, for example, games 3.9, 4.3, 7.22.

Learning styles

For some years now the idea that we all have different emphases in the way we perceive and learn has become part of every teacher's life. Learning styles are not considered to be exclusive. For example, the same person may sometimes want to be analytical and at other times may want to be creative. However, each person will probably have preferences. In any one class there can be many different preferences. The teacher is like a gardener responsible for many different types of plant, some requiring a lot of sunshine and others shade, some requiring pruning and others to be left alone. You can treat all your plants in the same way and watch some die while others flourish, or you can try to offer a range of different approaches and give succour to each and all of them. We have attempted to help you to do this by providing games involving a wide variety of learning styles, from 'visual' to 'dramatic'.

Visual
Some people respond best of all to information which is seen: pictures, writing, diagrams, etc. Note also: colour, size, design, etc. *'I see what you mean.'*

See, for example, games 2.1, 6.4, 6.6, 7.14.

Auditory
Other people might respond to information which is heard: dialogues, songs, rhythm, etc. *'I hear what you are saying.'*

See, for example, games 2.13, 3.3, 7.7, 7.25.

Kinaesthetic
Others might need to move and to touch in order to learn efficiently. *'I've put it together, at last.'*

See, for example, games 1.1, 5.1, 5.8, 6.1, 6.9.

Creative

Some people need to use the language creatively even from the beginning. *'Let's have a go.'*

See, for example, games 2.5, 2.9, 2.10, 2.11.

Analytical

Some people like to analyse language forms, looking for rules. Having understood the 'bricks' of the language then they might feel able, tentatively, to use them. *'Let's stop messing about and get down to the basic rules.'*

See, for example, games 2.4, 2.6, 3.7, 3.8, 7.18.

Cooperative

Some people like to work with others. *'It's really good fun to work with other people.'*

See, for example, games 1.2, 4.3, 4.12, 4.13.

Individual

Some people prefer to work by themselves. *'I like to be left alone to get on with it.'*

See, for example, games 2.12, 3.7, 3.9, 8.9.

Serious

Some people can concentrate better if the approach is serious. *'I don't want to mess about, but get down to the real business of learning.'*

See, for example, games 1.9, 5.4, 6.12, 6.14.

Amusing

Some people concentrate better if there is an element of humour and lightness in the experience. *'I like a good laugh.'* *'Don't take it all so seriously.'*

See, for example, games 4.7, 4.8, 7.2, 7.11, 7.24.

Dramatic

Some people experience and absorb language associated with drama and story telling. *'I love a good story.'*

See, for example, games 3.2, 4.4, 4.13, 8.17.

Real

Some people prefer to deal with real examples from everyday experience.
'*I want to prepare for the real world.*'
   See, for example, games 1.4, 2.8, 4.10, 6.13, 7.9.

Practicalities of organising games

Teachers experienced in using games in their teaching report the following,
for which we are very grateful:

General ideas on using games

'*Don't think that the use of the word "game" is a guaranteed way of
motivating the students. They are too sceptical. It must be a genuinely
engaging activity.*'
'*Don't tell the learners that they are going to play a game because they may
not accept that some of them are games and they may protest and be
distracted from a positive attitude to what should be a pleasurable
experience.*'

The importance of making the game clear

'*Find a way of demonstrating the game as well as explaining it, perhaps
demonstrating it with the class as a whole or with selected students so that
everybody can get the gist of it. It is essential that all the students know what
to do before you let them go into pair or group work.*'
'*It is particularly important to make sure everyone understands what to do
when the game is quite complicated!*'
'*Once the game starts it is difficult to help, so try putting helpful phrases on
the board or on an A2 poster.*'
'*Avoid games which need a long introduction and explanation. The students
will just turn off.*'

Mistakes

'*Of course, they may make mistakes when you are not there to correct them.
But the biggest mistake is not to speak at all, so group work and pair work
are essential.*'
'*Normally, don't interrupt a game in order to correct a mistake, but
comment on it afterwards or just make a note for yourself to do more
practice of that point at a future time.*'

'It is not the right time to correct mistakes of language during the game if that impedes the involvement of the students and the flow of the game. Correct mistakes later or, better, do activities which practise correct forms, later.'

Pair work and group work

'Pair work is easier to organise and control than group work.'
'If there is competition between groups then make sure that each group represents mixed ability.'

Determining the composition of pairs and groups

'People naturally choose to work with people they know well, but sometimes you might prefer them to be open to new working relationships. Ask the learners to stand in a line and then to go through the alphabet with A the first person, B the second, and so on. If you want to have five groups then the learners call out from A to E and then begin again at A. When this is completed you point to one part of the room and say, "All As over there. All Bs over here. All Cs, etc." In this way random groupings can be made quickly.'
'Think about group dynamics. Sometimes adding or removing one or two individuals from a group makes that group so much more productive.'

Success ... and particularly how to avoid failure

'The problem with some games is that they tend to make one person the winner and the rest losers. What we need in the classroom is for everybody to experience success as much as possible. Look for games or ways of playing games which allow for that.'
'Maximise ways of making every student experience success, for example, fewer games based on individuals playing against each other, and more based on team work.'
'Find the right level of game for the learners. This makes all the difference between success and failure.'

Justify the use of games

'When necessary, be prepared to justify the use of games to the students in terms of their efficiency: the frequency with which the language point occurs, meaningful use of the language, successful consequence if the language is used appropriately, memorability.'

Discipline

'Discipline is important but cannot be established by shouting, which, in any case, ruins the whole spirit created by enjoyable games. Here are some approaches which help discipline:

- *Establish a set of agreed general class rules at the beginning of the year. Write these discussed and agreed rules on a poster and keep it on the classroom wall.*
- *If you need to stop the class, use the technique of raising your hand rather than trying to shout over the hubbub of a game in progress. The raised hand spreads peace and the shout raises tensions.*
- *Make the procedure for playing the game very clear to ALL the students.*
- *Be seen to be very fair to everyone.'*

How to use this book

Level: In the grey panel at the head of each game we give the language point focussed on by the game and you are the best judge of which class and level of learner to use the game with.

Time: Most games in the book are likely to last from 10 to 20 minutes, but different classes and teachers need different amounts of time.

Material required: This important ingredient is included for each game under the heading **Preparation**.

Index

If you have a particular language point or function in mind, look in the Index to see which games focus on it.

1 Icebreakers and warmers

It is important for learners to feel comfortable with each other, confident in themselves and focussed on the language lesson rather than on other distractions. We would also like them to be creative, risk-taking, thoughtful, communicative, happy to work together with other learners. To help this situation to develop, the teacher can do 'icebreaker' games with a new class and 'warmers' at the beginning of a lesson with a class where the learners already know each other.

Games and 'playfulness' as a way of warming people and helping them to focus their minds are complemented by the way the classroom looks and how you greet them. Music playing, pictures on the walls, the furniture arranged attractively, curious objects, coloured cloths and smiling faces drawn on the board can all help to get the lesson off to a good start.

All the games in this chapter belong to the family of games of CARE AND SHARE. See Introduction, page 4.

CARE AND SHARE

1.1 Learning names

Family	CARE AND SHARE
Language	Introducing oneself and others, learning names
Variation	Sharing likes or other personal information, learning names
Preparation	Set a friendly classroom atmosphere by putting on some music, if you wish.

Procedure

1 Ask the learners to mill about, nodding and smiling, in a space in the classroom. It is an advantage if you can have some cheerful music playing and stop it when you want them to stop.

2 Ask them to stop in front of another learner and introduce themselves. You can demonstrate this.

Learner 1: *Hello, I am Lars.*
Learner 2: *Hello, I am Zakia.*

3   Let the learners mill again until you stop them and ask them to introduce themselves again.
4   You can add to the challenge by asking them to point at and name the other people they have already met. They can help each other to do this, if necessary. This is a very effective way of practising the paradigm of the present simple: *I am, he/she is.*

> Learner 1:   *She's Barbara and she's Yvonne and he's Harry. I'm Ferdinand.*

Variation 1   Getting to know each other

1   Sit the learners in circles of about eight.
2   Give the class a moment or two to choose something which is important to them and can be referred to in one or two words. You can begin as the model. Introduce yourself by saying, for example, *I'm Martine and I like playing football.*
3   The next learner in the circle repeats what the first learner said and adds his or her own information.

> Learner 1:   *You're Martine and you like football. I'm Rubino and I have a pet dog.*

4   The third learner repeats what the first two learners said and then adds his or her own information. And so it continues round the circle.

Examples of other types of information to add
Family, home area, job
Favourite thing to do when not working, favourite food
Reason for learning English, anxieties about learning English
Something really nice which has happened recently

---

5   To make it more challenging, the person who has just spoken should choose the next speaker by pointing at them. This may not be their neighbour, but someone sitting on the other side of the circle. In this way it is a little more difficult to remember the information.

Notes

•   You can focus on learning styles by asking the learners to relate their information about jobs and hobbies with likes and dislikes and an estimation of how good they are at each activity, and in this way *you* will learn something about their possible learning style preferences.

- Learning names is a necessary condition to establishing familiarity and trust and confidence in the other class members.
- In order to establish a true communicative classroom atmosphere you must include yourself in all of these activities.

1.2 Stand in a line

Family	CARE AND SHARE
Language	Interacting with others using minimal language
Preparation	Since this activity is based on the learners having to arrange themselves in a line according to a specified criterion, think of criteria you would like to use, for example: Names in alphabetical order Date of birth Favourite month Zodiac sign Favourite times of the day

Procedure

1 Ask the learners to form a line according to the criterion you have chosen, for example, in alphabetical order of their names. Tell them they should speak to each other in order to decide how to line up. For example:

Learner 1: *What's your name?*

Learner 2: *David.*

Learner 1: *Oh, you're before me. I must stand here. I'm Eva.*

2 Once the learners have formed a line, ask them to bend round into a circle and then say their names (or whatever criterion was used) in order.

3 Once you have got the learners into a circle, you might like to follow this up with the game below.

1.3 Pass on a sound

Family	CARE AND SHARE
Language	Repeating a sound, word or phrase exactly

Procedure

Ask the learners to form a circle. (You might like to do the game above to achieve this.) In order to build up a feeling of sharing and listening to each other you can now ask them to pass on a sound or a word or phrase. This requires the learners to pay close attention to each other in order to copy exactly what the other person is saying or doing.

> **Examples of sounds and phrases to pass on**
> *Ba! Ba! Ba! Ba! Baaaa! Ba!* (the fifth Ba spoken slowly and drawn out)
> *Hello.* (spoken very cheerfully)
> *I'm John.* (or any other sentence originated by the learner)

1.4 Questions and questionnaires

Family	CARE AND SHARE
Language	Getting to know others by asking questions
	Giving personal information by answering questions

Procedure

1   Explain to the learners that all of the games in the variations (below) are based on questions which are used to find out more about other people in the class.

2   Help the learners to brainstorm on to the board questions which they might ask a person whom they would like to get to know. For example:
What's your name?
Where do you live?
What's your job?
Have you got children?
What's your hobby?
What's your favourite food/music, etc?
Examples of more personal and demanding questions
Are you married?
What worries you?
What is your greatest fear?
What is your favourite type of holiday?
What would you do if you found a lot of money in a park?

3   Tell the learners to leave their seats, mill about, and put questions to at least three other people.

4   Finally, invite the class to sit in a circle, and ask each learner to describe a classmate using all the information gathered. The rest of the class should try to guess the person referred to.

Here are some different ways of organising this activity:

- The learners first choose a number of questions and write them on a questionnaire, and then ask their classmates questions to complete their questionnaires. (Or you could provide each learner with a questionnaire which you have written yourself.)
- The learners, sitting in pairs, put the questions to their partner.
- Learners in groups of three take it in turns to question and answer.
- Divide the class into two. Make an inner circle of learners facing outwards and an outer circle of learners facing inwards. The learners put their questions to the learner opposite. After about three minutes, tell the outer circle to move one place to the left, thus creating new pairs and allowing learners to repeat the same questions.
- Make two long rows of chairs facing each other. The learners put their questions to the learner opposite. After about three minutes, tell the learners on one row of chairs to move one chair to the left, thus creating new pairs. The learner at the end of the row must stand up and walk around to the other end of the line of chairs.

Variation 1   Questions about you

1   Ask learners each to write ten questions, the answers to which would be revealing of *their own* personality, interests and concerns.
2   Organise the class into pairs. Have the learners ask their partners the questions they have written. Allow learners to ask supplementary questions if desired.
3   Invite individual learners to tell the class what they have learned about their partner.

Variation 2   Predict your partner's answers

1   Ask each learner to devise and write down ten questions.
2   Put learners into pairs and ask each learner to write the answers they would expect their partner to give in response to the questions.
3   Finally, ask the learners to put their questions to their partners and compare the predicted answers with the actual answers.

Variation 3   Yes/No questions to the teacher

1   Encourage learners to ask you questions inviting *Yes* or *No* answers. Reply honestly!
2   If a learner gets *No* as an answer, then they must ask another question.

3   If a question is incorrect grammatically, wait for the other learners to help
    him or her to get it right.

    Learner 1:   *Are you liking sports?*
    Learner 2:   (corrects Learner 1) *Do you like sports?*
    Learner 1:   *Thanks. Do you like sports?*
    Teacher: *No.*
    Learner 1:   *Do you have a car?*
    Teacher: *Yes.*
    Learner 3:   *Do you ...?*

Variation 4   Questions to the teacher: what's the truth?

1   Draw three columns on the board.
2   Tell the learners to ask any questions they would like you to answer,
    providing that they only require a short answer.
3   Write three different answers to each question, two being false and one
    truthful. Write the truthful answers under the same column, but without
    giving any clue to the learners as to which one it is.
4   Ask the learners to work in groups and to discuss which set of
    answers they think is the 'real' you. Let them guess, then reveal the
    answer.
5   Invite the learners to play the same game in pairs or small groups.

1.5   Find someone who ...

Family	CARE AND SHARE
Language	Asking and answering questions to get information about peers
Variation	Finding out and reporting on what you have in common with other people
Preparation	Think of topics you would like the learners to explore.

Procedure

1   Write three or four instructions on the board. The conventional way of
    doing this is to use the phrase *Find someone who...*, for example, *Find
    someone who lives in the same neighbourhood as you.* However, you
    may prefer also to provide the learners with the actual questions they
    should use, for example, *Where do you live?*
    Alternatively, let the learners themselves choose the topics and formulate
    their own questions. Examples might be:

Find someone who lives near you.
Find someone who likes the same food as you.
Find someone who likes the same music as you.
Find someone who likes the same hobbies and pastimes as you.
Find someone who has the same reasons for, or anxieties about,
learning English as you.
Find someone who has a pet.
Find someone who has been to another country.

2   Ask the learners to walk about the room talking to each other and finding out the information you have specified.

Variation 1   Things in common

1   Have the learners work in groups to find out what they have in common. You may wish to provide some useful sentence starters or topics, for example:
    Have you got a …? / Do you have a …?
    Is your …?
    Do you like …?
    Can you …?
    Have you ever …?
    Learners may take notes.

2   Each learner should tell the class about one of the things the group members have in common, for example:
    All of us *have (got) a brother or a sister.*
    Most of us *live in the same district of the city.*
    Some of us *have a pet.*
    A few of us *can drive a car.*
    None of us *likes boring lessons.*
    We are grateful to Mario Rinvolucri for this example.

Note

You may wish to play this game in pairs, in which case learners should find out about ways in which they are similar to and different from their partner. Help the learners by showing them sentence starters such as the following:
    She/He …, but I …
    We both …
    Neither of us …

1.6 Match the person to the information

Family	CARE AND SHARE
Language	Using general descriptive language
	Getting to know others by hearing, reading, then trying to retrieve a piece of information about them
	Learning names
Preparation	Cut two strips of card or paper about 10 cm x 2 cm for each learner.

Procedure

1 Give the learners two cards each and ask them to write their name on one and a sentence about themselves on the other. For example:

Card 1: *DAVID.*

Card 2: *I like walking in the country and looking at nature.*

The name should be written in block capitals, so that the handwriting on the two cards cannot be easily matched. For the same reason it would also help to use a different pen for each card.

2 Put the learners into groups and have them take turns introducing themselves to the group and reading out their sentences.

3 Tell the learners to shuffle the group's cards together, then lay them out face down on a table.

4 The learners take turns to try to find matching pairs of cards. To do this, they turn two cards face up. If they think they have found a pair, they point at the relevant person and say, for example, *This is David. He likes walking in the country and looking at nature.* If they are correct, they keep the cards. If they are wrong, they turn them back on the table face down.

1.7 Topics to talk about

Family	CARE AND SHARE
Language	Using general language to talk about a familiar topic

Procedure

1 Ask learners to write down four topics related to themselves that they are willing to talk about, for example, *sport, hobby, family, job.*

2 Have learners form pairs and tell them to ask their partner questions about each topic. Their partner should answer as fully as they can. Allow about three minutes per topic.

3 Begin with yourself as a demonstration, if you wish, letting the class ask you questions about a topic you have chosen.

Variation 1 Something nice which happened

Ask pairs or groups of learners to take it in turns to tell each other about something nice which has happened to them recently.

Variation 2 A special object

Preparation Ask learners to bring a special personal possession to class.

1 Ask learners to form groups. Then each member of the group should put a personal possession on the table in front of them.
2 Encourage learners to take turns saying anything they can about their object and answering any questions put to them by the other members of their group.

Variation 3 A special number

1 Write a number on the board and tell the class why it is important to you. The number might be: a date, a telephone number, a lucky or unlucky number, the number of people in your family, the number of people in your favourite sport, etc.
2 Ask learners to do the same working with a partner.

Variation 4 A random word

1 Invite a learner to choose a letter between A and Z. Write it on the board, then ask the learners to call out nouns beginning with that letter. Write the nouns on the board, too.
2 Tell learners, working in pairs, each to choose one word and talk about it for three minutes.

Variation 5 A colour

1 Brainstorm on to the board colours the learners can name.
2 Ask each of the learners to pick a colour and to brainstorm, on paper, personal associations with that colour.
3 Tell the learners to share their associations with a partner.

1.8 All the words you know

Family	CARE AND SHARE
Language	Boosting the confidence of beginner learners by compiling a list of familiar English words

Procedure

1 Help the learners brainstorm on to the board all the English words they already know (English words used in their own language or words they know from general contact with the international use of English).

2 Challenge the learners to remember all the words by erasing them one by one, then asking the learners to reconstruct the list of words together orally.

Notes

• The primary aim is to help beginners or near beginners feel confident that they already know something, and to introduce them to the different sounds of English in contrast with those of their own mother tongue.

• Another aim is to begin to build a team effort.

• This game could have more of a cultural focus according to your questions, e.g. *Tell me the names of some famous British people … famous American cities,* etc.

1.9 Proverbs

Family	CARE AND SHARE
Language	Learning and using proverbs in everyday experience
Preparation	Photocopy a list of proverbs for each learner. Compile a list of proverbs from the learners' own culture and look for English equivalents, or list some English proverbs and be prepared to explain them.

Procedure

1 Share the list of proverbs with the learners and ensure that the meaning of each is understood by demonstrating how it applies to everyday experience.

2 Ask each learner to learn at least one of the proverbs and then use it whenever the opportunity arises during the lesson.

> **Examples of proverbs**
> *Nothing ventured, nothing gained.*
> *Experience is the best teacher.*
> *Don't judge a book by its cover.*
> *A change is as good as a rest.*
>
> *Rome wasn't built in a day.*
> *All work and no play makes Jack a dull boy.*
> *Never say die.*

Note

Proverbs can be learned in each lesson and at every level. They are satisfying at the beginner level because it is a big thing learned. For more proverbs see *The Oxford Book of Proverbs*, Oxford University Press.

1.10 Jog! Jog!

Family	CARE AND SHARE
Language	Recognising and carrying out instructions (i.e. imperatives) requiring a physical response

Procedure

1 Have the learners stand together in an open space.
2 Tell them to follow your instructions, repeating the verb over and over as they do so. The first instruction – and every second instruction throughout the game – is one that makes the learners circulate: *Jog!*

Teacher:	(starts jogging around the room) *Jog! Jog! Jog!* etc.
Learners:	(jogging) *Jog! Jog! Jog!* etc.
Teacher:	(stops jogging) *Pat your neighbour's head!* (turns to the closest person and starts patting their head) *Pat! Pat! Pat!* etc.
Learners:	(patting their neighbour's head) *Pat! Pat! Pat!* etc.
Teacher:	(stops patting and starts jogging around the room) *Jog! Jog! Jog!* etc.
Learners:	(jogging) *Jog! Jog! Jog!* etc.

Other instructions: *touch, tap, stroke, tickle, slap, scratch.*

Note

We fully appreciate that making bodily contact is not considered appropriate in some cultures and with some individuals. As with all games in this book we consider that the teacher knows what is acceptable.

Acknowledgement

We first experienced this game with Nick Owen at Pilgrims, then saw it developed by Julia Dudas at International Languages Institute, Hungary.

1.11 Visualisation

Family	CARE AND SHARE
Language	Recognising and mentally carrying out instructions (i.e. imperatives) and using oral descriptions to create mental images
Preparation	Find or prepare a visualisation script. (See the example in step 3 below.)

Most people can see pictures in their minds, particularly when the pictures are described. At the beginning of a class, a visualisation activity can help the learners to relax and focus on their work in the lesson ahead, and it emphasises both pleasure and success.

Procedure

1   Introduce the idea of relaxing, with the learners looking at you as you speak, and act out the idea of relaxing. Say (and act), for example:
    Relax. Take two deep breaths and relax all of your body: your feet, your legs, your stomach and chest, your arms and wrists and hands. Relax your neck and your face …
2   When you feel the learners have got the idea of relaxing, ask them to put their heads on their arms, close their eyes and relax as they listen.
3   Describe a situation for the learners to imagine, for example:
    You are walking in the country. There are trees and flowers and grass. It is very quiet; there are no people or cars. You are carrying a bag. It is on your back. It is heavy. You want to sit down. Take off your bag. Put it down. Sit on the grass. It's nice. You are happy. Open your bag. Look inside. Are your things in the bag? Now, close the bag. Look. Is it closed? Put your bag in a safe place. Now you can walk again. There is no bag on your back. How do you feel now? Enjoy your walking,

*slowly or quickly. It's OK to walk slowly. It's OK to walk quickly.
What can you see? What can you hear? What can you feel and smell?
Leave your bag. You will go back later. How do you feel? Keep those
feelings. Slowly open your eyes. Open your eyes.*

Further reading

Hall, E., Hall, C., and Leech, A. *Scripted Fantasy in the Classroom*,
    Routledge, 1990.
This book contains many useful examples of visualisation scripts.

1.12 Lost in the fog

Family	CARE AND SHARE
Language	Giving and carrying out instructions (i.e. imperatives) requiring a physical response
Preparation	Clear an area of floor space in the room and place a number of small objects or pieces of card here and there, representing hazardous rocks and shallows in an imaginary sea.

Procedure

1   Ask each learner to choose a partner. One person in each pair should be
    the ship's pilot, the other should be the on-shore coastguard.
2   Invite a number of pairs to play. It is a matter of judgement how many –
    or how few – pairs you choose to have on the floor at any one time. The
    ship's pilots must keep their eyes shut, simulating the problem of being in
    thick fog without radar. The coastguards must talk to the pilots by 'radio'
    and attempt to guide them safely through the hazards and into the
    'harbour'. The following phrases, which may be written on the board,
    will prove useful:
    Go forward.
    Stop.
    Turn left/right.
    Straight on.
    A bit further.
    Careful.

2 Mainly speaking

The games in this section offer a reason for speaking, and thus they can give learners a confirmation and confidence resulting from the successful use of the language or a warning signal on the unsuccessful use of the language.

Some games give the learners considerable support in the language needed for the game, and other games offer a stimulus and context, but no specific language focus or support. Although some games are likely to cause the learners to focus on a particular language point, this section primarily offers practice in fluency rather than in grammar practice.

In these games the learners might make mistakes in their use of the language. As a general principle it is better not to interrupt the speaker but to wait until he or she has finished before first responding to the content, and only then pointing out a mistake in the formal use of the language, if you think it necessary to do so. A better way might be for you to note the mistake and to give focussed practice on that point at another time.

IDENTIFY: *DISCRIMINATE, GUESS, SPECULATE*

2.1 Slowly reveal a picture

Family	IDENTIFY: *SPECULATE*
Language	Speculating about the contents of a partially obscured picture using expressions of uncertainty (e.g. *I think it is a ...*) and certainty (e.g. *It's a ...*) Using particular vocabulary or language points (as determined by the teacher's choice of picture)
Preparation	You will need a picture (drawn or from a magazine) which is big enough for the class to see (A4 size is usually big enough) and an envelope or a book to pull it out of.

Procedure

1 Put a picture, for example, a magazine picture, in an envelope or hide it in a book.
2 Pull out a very small part of the picture and ask the learners to try to identify it.

3 Pull out a little more of the picture and ask the learners what they think it is now. Ask them to tell their neighbour what they think it is. This makes everyone participate by using the language and expressing their view.
4 Gradually show more and more of the picture. Encourage the drama of different opinions.

2.2 Liar!

Family	IDENTIFY: *DISCRIMINATE*
Language	**Main game** Describing and answering questions about real and imagined pictures
	Questioning others with the aim of determining honesty and exposing lies
	Variation Scanning spoken text for untrue elements.
Preparation	You will need 4 file folders: 3 containing pictures, 1 containing a blank sheet of paper.

Procedure

1 Give the file folders to four volunteers and invite them to look at what is inside, being careful not to reveal it to anyone.
2 Have the four volunteers take turns giving a truthful description of their picture, except for the volunteer with the blank paper, who should invent a convincing description of an imaginary picture in an attempt to fool the class.
3 Encourage the rest of the learners to ask the four volunteers questions in an effort to expose the 'liar'.
4 Let the class vote on who they think was the 'liar', then have the four volunteers reveal the contents of their folders.

Variation 1 You're pulling my leg!

Preparation	Think up a tall tale to tell learners (or invent one spontaneously as you are playing the game, if you are comfortable doing so).

Procedure

1 Discuss the idea that there are always people who like to 'pull other people's legs', i.e. make them look a little foolish. Explain that this game will train the learners not to have their legs pulled! Explain that you will talk and include a few untrue statements. The learners must immediately raise their hands on hearing an untrue statement and say what is wrong with it. For example:

> Teacher *or* Learner 1: *Yesterday I went into town and saw a beautiful car. It had six legs and went very …*
>
> Learner 2: *That's not true. Cars don't have legs, they have wheels. And they don't have six wheels, they have four wheels.*
>
> Teacher: *Oh, sorry. You're quite right. Anyway, it was going very fast. I went to the chemist's to buy some bread …*
>
> Learner 3: *You can't buy bread at the chemist's.*

2 Once the idea of the game is understood, play it in groups or in pairs. Learners might prepare their own 'talk' in writing, perhaps for homework.

Notes

- 'To pull someone's leg' means to tell them something that isn't true as a way of joking with them.
- 'Tall stories', entailing unlikely exaggeration, are a traditional form of story in both the oral and the written traditions of storytelling. Baron von Munchausen is one of the best known tellers of tall stories.

DESCRIBE

2.3 Describe and draw

Family	DESCRIBE
Language	Describing a drawing and reproducing it by following instructions Giving and following instructions using imperatives, prepositions of location, adjectives and comparatives of adjectives, vocabulary for shapes, and possibly specialised language
Preparation	You will need a picture or a drawing on paper or OHP transparency of a few quite simple and clearly defined objects (preferably not people). Use a technical drawing if you wish to focus on specialised language.

Procedure

1 Ask a volunteer to stand by the board. Then display a large picture which all the class can see, except the volunteer by the board. For example, the picture can be displayed on a movable board. If necessary the picture can be held up by two learners.

2 Invite the class to describe the picture and tell the volunteer how to draw it. Explain that the aim is to help the artist to make a good copy of the

picture. It is helpful to begin with a general description. Here is an example.

Teacher: *What's the shape of the picture?*

Learner 1: *It's a rectangle.*

Teacher: *Artist, please draw a rectangle ... a long rectangle.*

(The artist draws the rectangle. The class can call out for him or her to make it longer or shorter.)

Teacher: *What is in the picture?*

Class: *A house ... a tree ... two people ... a dog ... some birds.*

Teacher: *OK. Now, is the line for the garden near the top of the picture, in the middle or near the bottom of the picture?*

Learner 2: *Near the bottom of the picture.*

Teacher: *OK, Artist, draw a line near the bottom of the picture ... a long, straight line. OK. Now the house. What shape is it?*

Learner 3: *It's a rectangle.*

Teacher: *Is it a long rectangle or a tall rectangle?*

Learner 4: *It's a tall rectangle.*

Teacher: *And where is the house?*

Learner 5: *It's in the middle of the picture.*

Teacher: *OK. Artist, draw a tall rectangle in the middle of the picture.*

Note

In the example given above, the teacher plays a major part. This is in order to provide a model both for how to communicate clearly and helpfully, and for the sort of language which might be required.

Variation 1 Describe and draw in pairs

Preparation	You will need a picture or a drawing on paper or OHP transparency of a few quite simple and clearly defined objects (preferably not people).

1 Have learners sit in pairs in such a way that only one of them can see the picture you have put on display, or provide a photocopy of a picture (perhaps the same picture) for each pair.
2 Ask one partner in each pair to describe the picture to the other, giving instructions on how to make an accurate reproduction. The artist must not see the original. The describer can see both the original and the copy being made. Or, to make the game more challenging, have the learners sit back to back so that the describer cannot see the copy being made!

Notes

- If each describer uses a copy of the same picture, then all the artists' pictures can be compared.
- It is an art in itself to describe a picture so that someone else can draw it. It is better to do this game as a class game first of all in order to help to teach the learners the art of describing and the necessary language for it. Here are some tips:
  Give the artist an overview first of all, for example, *It's a picture of a house, a tree, some flowers, a garden gate*, etc.
  Tell the artist the basic shape of the frame, for example, *The picture is a rectangle. It is a tall rectangle* [i.e. portrait format] *not a long one* [i.e. not landscape format].

- This is a classic 'information gap' game of the communicative approach in which one person has the information which the other hasn't got and needs. Language is used to bridge the gap.
- This game represents a communal effort and there is absolutely no reason why the artist should feel humiliated if their drawing does not turn out well. Indeed much of the success or otherwise of the artist's drawing is the result of the quality of communicative competence of the describers.

2.4 Describe and identify

Family	DESCRIBE
Language	Using descriptive language and vocabulary as determined by the teacher's choice of words or pictures
	Main game Defining words
	Variations 1 and 2 Describing images
	Variation 3 Scripting a conversation between two characters
	Variation 4 Imagining a character's thoughts and putting them on paper
Preparation	Write a single word on a number of small cards or pieces of paper, one per learner, plus a few extra. The words are going to be described by the learners well enough for the other learners to identify what has been described.

Procedure

1 Demonstrate the idea of this game by describing something and asking the class to identify what you have described. The subject and language you use should be appropriate to the learners' level of proficiency and the language you want to practise with them.

2 Rather than allowing the learners to call out, ask them first to tell their neighbours what they think you have described. Then ask for suggestions from the class.

3 Ask one of the more confident learners to take one of the word cards at random from your hand. He or she must describe the meaning of the word on the card so well that others can identify what it is.

4 Give each learner a card and instruct them to prepare a written description of the word on the card. This task is ideal for homework.

Examples

Cat: *It's an animal. It has four legs and a tail. It says miaow. It eats mice.*
Town Hall: *It's the place where the local government of the town have their offices.*

---

5 Ask all the learners to stand up, mill about, read their description to five other learners, and note down how often their listener can accurately identify the thing described.
6 Ask some or all of the learners to read out their descriptions to the whole class.

Variation 1 Describe and identify a picture

Preparation   Bring a number of pictures to the lesson.

1 Ask one learner to describe a particular picture from a choice of at least five which everyone can see.
2 Encourage his or her partner or group or the rest of the class to identify which picture has been described.

Variation 2 Describe and identify a detail in a picture

Preparation   Bring several pictures or a picture with many people and/or objects in it.

1 Ask one learner to think of a person or an object in a/the picture and then describe him, her or it.
2 Encourage the rest of the class to identify the person or object which has been described.

Variation 3 Describe and identify a conversation in a picture

Preparation   Bring a large picture with a lot of people in it, or several different pictures of people interacting.

1 Show the picture(s) to the class and ask them to work in pairs. Explain that they have to choose two people in the picture who might be having a conversation. The pairs should not reveal their choice to others in the class.
2 Ask each pair to devise and write out a conversation between the chosen characters, and perform it for the rest of the class.

3 Invite the class to identify which two characters were being represented in each conversation.

Variation 4 Describe and identify thoughts in a picture

Preparation	Bring a large picture with a lot of people in it or several different pictures of people.

1 Show the picture(s) to the learners and ask each of them to choose one character, without revealing their choice to anyone else.
2 Ask each learner to write what their chosen character might be thinking in the picture, then to read his or her text to the rest of the class.
3 Invite the learners to identify which person was being represented in each case.

Notes

- An ideal picture for Variations 2, 3 and 4 would be the famous Bruegel painting of children playing 90 different games.
- Comic strips are good sources of pictures for all of the variations. So are pictures you might already have hanging on your classroom walls.
- You may wish to make the game more challenging by requiring the learners to ask questions to gather information, rather than having them listen to prepared descriptions.

CONNECT: *COMPARE, MATCH, GROUP*

2.5 Two pictures

Family	CONNECT
Language	Imagining and explaining connections between pictures, objects or words
Preparation	You will need two pictures big enough for all the learners to see, each showing a single object, person or place.

Procedure

1 Take two seemingly unrelated pictures and ask the learners to suggest a connection between them. Some learners will suggest very reasonable connections. Some learners will suggest crazy connections. In one sense, the latter are more useful since more people will pay attention and think about them!

Example:
    Learner 1: *She's going to the bank to get some money.*
    Learner 2: *She's going to the bank to steal some money.*
    etc.
2   If you wish, organise a competition to find the most reasonable
    connection and the craziest connection.

Note

This game may be played in groups or with the whole class.

 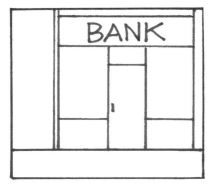

Variation 1 Three words

Preparation   (optional) Bring 3 objects to the lesson.

Procedure

1   Show the class three objects or write three nouns on the board, for
    example, *pencil, ball, table.*
2   Invite learners to find as many things as possible which might connect
    them, for example:
        *The **pencil** and **ball** are on the **table**.*
        or:
        *She does her homework on the **table** and she uses a **pencil**. Then she
        plays table tennis on the **table** and uses a table tennis **ball**.*

2.6 What's the difference?

Family Language	CONNECT: *COMPARE* Describing and comparing pictures or other types of visual input Using different language items, depending on the pictures chosen, for example: **Nouns** *In John's picture there are three animals: an elephant, a dog and a crocodile. In Helen's picture there are four animals: an elephant, a cat, a crocodile and a snake.* **Colours** *In the first picture the walls are pink, and in the second picture the walls are blue.* **Comparisons** *In one picture the monkey's thumb is longer than in the other picture.* **Tenses** *In one picture the man is going to fall, and in the other picture he has already fallen.*
Preparation	For each pair of learners, you will need two pictures or sets of pictures which are very similar but contain several differences which the learners will be able to describe. **Possible sources and types of picture** a) Magazine or catalogue pictures: for example, two pictures of different though similar bathrooms, or houses, or articles of clothing. b) A line drawing, perhaps from a magazine. Photocopy the drawing, then white out some parts. You can draw in alternative bits if you wish. Then photocopy the altered photocopy. In this way you will have two very similar drawings but with interesting small differences. c) Instead of *one* pair of drawings, you can have a lot of them. And instead of being, for example, naturalistic representations, they can be *very* simple or even abstract designs. *Ten* such pictures fit on to one sheet of A4. (See illustration on next page.) d) Of course *any* information which is similar, though not identical, may be used. The information may be verbal or numerical instead of pictorial. It *could* be all three!

Procedure

1 Divide the class into pairs.
2 Provide each player with one picture and warn everyone not to look at their partner's picture.

3 Tell learners that both players should describe their own picture and/or ask questions about their partner's picture, with the aim of finding the differences between the two pictures.

4 Finally, let the learners look at each other's pictures and compare and discuss further.

Variation 1 Comparing pictures

1 Put learners into pairs and give a copy of picture A to each Learner A, and a copy of picture B to each Learner B.

2 Start play as in the main game, with partners describing and comparing their pictures orally.

3 After two minutes, ask Learner B from each pair to move to another Learner A.

4 Have the new pairs compare their conclusions concerning the similarities and the differences between their two pictures, then continue to try to find more.

5 After a further two minutes, ask the learner who moved before, to move again. Repeat step 4. And so on.

2.7 Find a connection

Family	CONNECT
Language	Arguing a connection between two cards
Preparation	You will need a set of cards for each group, such as the ones used in Pelmanism (see games 5.5, 6.9 and 7.16).

Procedure

1 Divide the class into groups of about four and give each group a set of cards.

2 The first player starts with one card, merely identifying it with a word or phrase. They can then choose any other picture card and keep it if they can argue a connection between the first card and the other one.

3 The group must decide if the idea is reasonable.

4 The game finishes when there are no more cards.

5 The group must then try to argue why all the cards are related in one way or another to all the other cards!

REMEMBER

2.8 What can you remember?

Family	REMEMBER
Language	Describing things one recalls seeing, for example:
	There's a ...
	There are some ...
	There aren't any ...
	He/She's wearing ...

Procedure

1 Tell the class not to turn around.

2 Ask them what they think is behind them. They might refer to other people in the class, furniture, pictures on the walls, windows, etc. Ask for descriptions of the things they mention. Alternatively, you might ask what the learners can remember of the view through the window, for example, the street outside the school:

> Teacher: *Think about the street outside the school. What can you remember?*
>
> Learner 1: *There are some trees ...*
>
> Teacher: *Yes. Are there trees on both sides of the street?*
>
> Learner 1: *No, there aren't any on the other side.*
>
> Learner 2: *Yes, there are! There's one by the grocer's.*

Note

You may feel it is more profitable to let the learners look at or visit the selected place, object or person before the game takes place. You yourself might want to do this anyway.

Variation 1 What were they wearing?

1 Before you explain the game to the class, ask two of them to go outside the classroom.

2 Explain to the class that they have to describe from memory what the two outside are wearing. You could write on the board a summary of what they say.

3 Ask the two outside to come back in so that you can all check the accuracy of the class's description.

Variation 2 What is my neighbour wearing?

Ask a learner to close his or her eyes and describe his or her neighbour's appearance. Alternatively, the learners could stand back to back.

Variation 3 Can you remember the picture?

Preparation	Bring a picture to the lesson.

Challenge learners' memory by asking individuals to stand with their back to a picture which previously all of the class have been given time to look at. Invite the rest of the class, who are still looking at the picture, to ask the individuals questions about it.

CREATE

2.9 Stories with ten pictures

Family	CREATE
Language	Making up stories, using all the language at the learners' command, particularly past tense verb forms
Preparation	You will need approximately 10 pictures cut randomly from magazines. *Any* pictures will do, but they should show a variety of places and objects and include several people.
	If the pictures are big enough for all learners to see, put them up on the wall of the classroom. If not, provide one photocopy of the pictures for each pair or group of learners.
	Number the pictures.

Procedure

1 Ask pairs or groups to invent a story, making use of the pictures *in whatever order* most appeals to them. The number of the picture which corresponds to each part of the text must be written next to that text.

2 When everyone has finished, help the learners to share their stories by telling them to each other, writing and publishing them in a class book, putting them on the web, or displaying them on the wall.

Notes

• The advantage of all the groups using the same pictures is that each group will be interested to find out what the others have written and to compare the different versions.

- The advantage of publishing or performing a story is that it gives experience in using language for real purposes and pride in being able to do so.

Variation 1 Adding to a story

Preparation	You will need one picture or object for each learner.

1 Give a picture or an object to each learner.
2 Tell the learners that they will create a story together in the following manner: one learner (or the teacher) will start the story, then the next will continue where the previous person left off, and so on. Each learner must refer to the picture or object in front of them at some point in their portion of the story.

Variation 2 Silly news reports

1 Discuss with the learners the kinds of subjects which are reported on the television or radio news or in newspapers and list these subjects on the board.
2 Now ask each learner (or pair of learners) to write a *completely ludicrous* news report.
3 Ask each pair to read out their news.

Variation 3 Tour and tell

Preparation	You will need 5 or 6 small objects or pictures per group of learners, or 10 bigger pictures for the whole class to use. If you are using bigger pictures, put them up on the classroom wall.

1 Give the pictures or objects to the groups of learners, or tell them to look at the pictures on the wall.
2 Ask each group to invent a story based on the objects or pictures.
3 When the stories are ready, ask the learners to study their group's story so they will be able to tell it to others.
4 When this has been achieved, let the learners mill about and tell their group's story to at least three individual learners from other groups and also listen to their stories.

Notes

- You can add variety by specifying that the stories must be told through different media, for example, orally, as a book or a poster, on the school website, as a play to be videoed, as a play to be recorded on audio tape. Each of these types of story should then be displayed or performed for other people to enjoy. This goal of displaying and performing is very motivating and makes the learners want to get the language right.

- You can introduce further variety and increase the demands on the learners by asking them to tell their stories as if they were telling them to a certain type of listener, for example, a young child, an elderly person, a policeman, a friend, a teacher, a doctor, an employer, a customer. Some of these will be appropriate, some may not.

2.10 Question stories

Family	CREATE
Language	Using as wide a range of language as possible to create and tell a story in the present tense – and to retell it in the past tense – guided by questions (**main game**), pictures (**Variation 1**), objects (**Variation 2**), or a word or phrase (**Variation 3**)

Procedure

1 Tell the learners that they are going to make a story and you are going to help by asking questions. Tell them that anything you ask about must be included in the story.

2 Ask questions such as the following:
  Who is in your story? A man? A woman? A boy? A girl? An animal?
  (Then ask a few details about the person they choose.)
  Where is he/she/it at the beginning of the story?
  (Ask them to be precise even to a particular location, for example: *On the lowest branch of a big tree in a park in the middle of a city.*)
  When does the story begin? (season, month, day, time)
  What is the weather like?
  What is he/she doing?

3 Follow by using a variety of questions in order to help the drama to unfold, for example:
  What's he/she/it doing now?
  Something happens. What is it?
  Some people are watching him/her. Who are they? What do they want?

Notes

- You can collect the story in the present tense.
- Every five minutes you retell the story using past tenses.
- The following day you can ask the class to reconstruct and retell the story.

Variation 1   Question stories based on pictures

Preparation	You will need many calendar-sized pictures of people, places, etc. Display the pictures on the classroom wall.

1 Show the pictures to the learners. Tell them that these pictures are illustrations for their story, and that they must make a story to fit the pictures.
2 Use the same question technique as above.

Variation 2   Question stories based on objects

Preparation	You will need a collection of objects.

1 Show the objects to the learners. Ask them to make a story inspired by the objects.
2 Use the same question technique as above.

Variation 3   Question stories based on a single word or phrase

1 Write a single noun or verb on the board. Tell the learners that they must make up a story based on the word.
2 Use the same question technique as above, for example:
> **Starting word:** woman
> *What does this woman look like?*
> *What is she doing?*
> *Where is she?*
> *What's her problem?*
> etc.

Examples of starting phrases
She's crying.
It was very valuable.
The wind was blowing.
There was silence.

Notes

- This technique of storymaking can be used, and used profitably, at any level.
- It is better if you, as teacher, keep control of the collecting and retelling of the stories in order to keep the momentum of the drama going. However, students can be asked to retell the story, for example, the next day.
- The story can be retold or dramatised and recorded on audio or video tape. Simple audio effects make a vivid contribution to the drama of the story. It can be made into a written and illustrated book or put on the school website.

2.11 What can you do with it?

Family	CREATE
Language	Brainstorming possible uses of objects using *can* (positive) and *could* (tentative)
Preparation	You will need a collection of objects (optional, see step 1).

Procedure

1 Reveal a small collection of objects to the learners or write a list of objects on the board, for example, *a paper bag, a hammer, a pram, an empty tin can, a mirror, a table.*
2 Ask the learners to imagine different things which could be done with the objects, for example:

Teacher: *How can you use a paper bag?*
Learner 1: *You can put things in it.*
Teacher: *Yes, what else can you do with a paper bag?*
Learner 2: *You can light a fire with it.*
Teacher: *Yes. Anything else?*
Learner 3: *You can blow in it and then make a bang!*
Teacher: *Lovely! What else?*
Learner 4: *You could make it into a ball and throw it at someone to attract their attention!*

Notes

- You might find it supports the learners if you write key phrases on the board:
  You can ...
  You could ...

Or more extended sentence patterns:
You can/could make ... with it.
- This game works best if you encourage fun and invention.

2.12 What would you take?

Family	CREATE
Language	Expressing condition using *would*
	Explaining reasons for choices

Procedure

1 Tell the students that they will be stranded on a desert island (or locked in prison, or isolated in a hospital room) for one full year, and may only bring five items with them.
2 Give the learners a few minutes to make their list.
3 Invite learners to discuss their list with a neighbour, then a neighbouring pair, being sure to give the reasons for their choices. For example,
    Learner: **If I was going to be stranded on a desert island, I would bring** matches so I could start a fire for cooking and keeping warm.
    You may wish to write the starter phrase (in bold above) on the board.
4 Open the discussion to the class as a whole.

Note

The element of discussion means that this is more than a focussed vocabulary game.

2.13 A sound poem

Family	CREATE
Language	Exploring stress, pitch, tenor, and rhythm of syllables in creative
	combinations of words for *food*

Procedure

1 Help the learners to brainstorm on the board all the words they know for food.
2 Say one of the words and revel in its sound as you might revel in its taste. Emphasise or even exaggerate each sound in the words, for example *soup – ssssoooop!*

3 Ask *Which is your favourite food?* Encourage the learners to revel in the sounds of the words they choose.

4 Gradually help the learners to put some words or phrases together to make a 'sound poem'. Ask one half of the class to say one phrase and the other half of the class to say another phrase. Help them to enjoy the rhythm, speed and sound of the syllables working together. Keep in mind that rhyming is not necessary.

Example of a very simple 'sound poem'
Fish and chips (emphasising the crisp rhythm)
Fish and chips
Soup (extending the 'ou' sound)
Soup

---

5 Invite each learner to write a food poem supported by the words for food written on the board. Then ask them to try it out on other learners.

6 Finally, ask the learners to form groups, and make and perform a poem together for the rest of the class.

3 Mainly listening

Sometimes we listen for the gist of what the other person is saying and sometimes we listen for a particular detail of information that interests us. Sometimes the speaker's meanings are explicit, but at other times the meanings are implicit, and we must use our wits and imagination to catch the implications.

Responses to a text may be objective (for example, summarising the text or making an objective valuation of it) or may be subjective (for example, responding with personal ideas, feelings or associations).

When a learner's response to a text entails speaking or writing, it may be difficult for us to judge if his or her inadequacies in speaking and writing also mean inadequacies in listening. Furthermore, learners might be able to focus better on listening if they are not required to make an oral or written response. For these reasons we include games in this section that call for a non-verbal response, that is to say, 'listen and do'. The 'doing' shows, in a fair and accurate way, the extent to which the learner has listened, and understood.

DO: *MOVE, MIME, DRAW, OBEY*

3.1 Listen and draw

Family	DO: *DRAW*
Language	Listening for detail in the description of a person, object, animal or place and drawing according to the details described
	Possibly describing an imagined person, object, animal or place using descriptive language
Preparation	Write a description of a person, object, animal or place, keeping in mind that the learners will be asked to draw it.
	Make an enlarged copy of the description to display.

Procedure

1 Read a description of a person, object, animal or place. First of all, ask the learners to listen to the whole description without drawing. For example:

Teacher: *My neighbour is a very tall, thin woman. She wears a T-shirt. She wears narrow trousers. She has big feet, very big feet. And she wears big black boots. She has a square face and a long, pointed nose. She has two small eyes right in the middle of her face. She is always miserable and she has a long, miserable mouth. She has a lot of hair. She never combs her hair. It is full of birds. She has long thin arms and she always carries her little cat in her arms.*

2   Then read the description again, slowly, and ask the learners to draw what you describe. You may decide to encourage the learners to ask you questions for more clarity. Be willing to read the description several times.

We suggest that the learners draw in pencil until they are sure they have made a very accurate drawing. When they are sure, they may use a thin, black pen.

3   Display all the pictures drawn by the learners and display an enlarged copy of the text you have used. Check the pictures against the text to see if the details are correct.

45

4   Let the class vote for the top five most accurate pictures.
5   Consider asking the learners to do a similar activity in pairs or groups. For example, each pair of learners can be asked to describe, in writing, a subject that they can then describe to another pair for them to draw. Descriptions and pictures can then be displayed.

Notes

- This is a classic 'communication game'. There is an information gap: the speaker has the information and the learner does not, and must listen to understand it. The drawing shows, non-verbally, how well he or she has understood.
- If the teacher describes, then it is a listening game for the learners, but if the learners describe, it is also a speaking game. The art of describing is a very necessary art in daily life.
- For games in which the learners take on the speaking role, see pages 26 to 31.
- The tall thin woman and the animal could both provide the starting point for a fantasy set of characters and stories. See **4.13 Create a soap opera**.

Some other subjects which might be used for describing and drawing
a street map on which learners have to write the names of the streets and key buildings
a plan of a bedroom on which learners have to write the names of furniture and other objects
a fantasy machine, e.g. a machine for exercising dogs, which learners have to describe in detail
an abstract drawing in response to a poem
a diagram showing a technique or process
a graph or chart showing statistics

3.2 Act out a story

Family	DO: *MOVE*
Language	Responding through action to what is said
Preparation	Think of a story or situation in which actions play a major part.

Procedure

1 Ask the learners to sit in a circle, if you have enough room. Otherwise, they may remain at their desks.

2 Tell a story in which actions play a major part, and encourage the learners to act it out. For example:

> Teacher: *You've got a little cat in a box. Put the box on your desk. Say, 'Sit still. Don't move.' Now stroke the little cat and say, 'You're a nice cat.' Take the cat out of the box, very carefully and slowly. Put it down. Give it some milk in a saucer. Don't spill it! Say, 'Do you like the milk?' Stroke the cat again. Now say, 'Come on, little cat. Let me put you in the box.' Pick up the cat carefully and put it back in the box. Say, 'Stay there. Go to sleep. Go to sleep, little cat.'*
>
> *Show your friend your little cat. Tell her what it's like and what it is doing.*

Note

This is a version of the classic TPR (Total Physical Response) game which is recommended particularly for the early stage of language learning and particularly, though not exclusively, for younger learners.

IDENTIFY: *DISCRIMINATE, GUESS, SPECULATE*

3.3 Listen for the difference

Family	IDENTIFY: *DISCRIMINATE*
Language	Listening for differences in a spoken text as compared to a written one
Preparation	You will need a text on an OHP transparency or one photocopy of a text for each learner. Alternatively, choose a text from the learners' textbook.

Procedure

1 Begin by asking the learners to look at the text you have chosen. Then say that you will read the text to them, but because you are tired you might make some mistakes when you read it, and they must tell you if you do.

2 Read out the text and deliberately change some of it as you read. The learners should follow their copy of the text and immediately stop you when they notice one of the changes you have made. They must put up their hands and correct you.

3 Pretend that you are very tired or can't see very well and apologise profusely, but then continue and say things wrongly again a moment later. For example:

Teacher: *It was raining and ...*

Learner 1:   *It was snowing!*

Teacher: *Oh, I'm sorry. Yes. It was snowing and the wind was blowing. John was very cold ...*

Learner 2:   *John was cold, not very cold.*

Teacher: *Oh, dear, dear, dear. You are right. I need some new glasses. John was cold and ...*

4 Once the game is understood, let students play it in groups or pairs.

Variation 1 What's wrong?

1 Tell a story (or describe a place or a situation or an experience) known to the learners and change some of the information.

2 The learners listen for *information* being changed rather than individual *words* being changed, as in the main game.

Example of fact, misrepresentation and correction
Fact
The class had their annual fancy dress party on the previous Friday and the teacher came as a witch ...
Misrepresentation by the teacher
Last Thursday the fourth year classes had a Christmas party...
Correction by a student
It wasn't the fourth year classes, it was our class, and it was a fancy dress party, and it was on Friday...

Note

For other examples of well-known true/false games see 3.4, 4.1.

3.4 Repeat it if it is true

Family	IDENTIFY: *DISCRIMINATE*
Language	Evaluating the accuracy of oral statements about images
	Selecting statements to repeat after the teacher
Preparation	You will need 10–15 pictures big enough to be seen the length of the classroom.
	When choosing your pictures, keep in mind that each one should emphasise a single concept, e.g.
	running, swimming, climbing
	has got … / hasn't got …
	some, any
	in, on, under, next to

Procedure

1 Hold up one of the pictures and make a true or false statement about it. The class should listen and repeat what you have said, *if it is true*.

2 You can have a competition with the class. Give yourself a point every time you can get the class to repeat something that is untrue, and give the class a point when they respond correctly (by repeating something true or ignoring something false). If you feel it is potentially discouraging to hold a single learner responsible for losing a point for the class, then you might say that three or more learners must make a mistake in order for the class to lose a point.

> Teacher: (holding up a picture of someone running) *He's running.*
> Class: *He's running.*
> Teacher: *That's one point for you.*
> Teacher: (holding up a picture of someone reading) *She's swimming.*
> Class: (The learners refuse to speak because it is not a picture of swimming.)
> Teacher: *Another point for you.*

Note

You might like to play the game twice using exactly the same material to see if the class score improves.

3.5 Which picture is it?

Family	IDENTIFY
Language	Listening to descriptive language with the aim of identifying what is being described
	Describing a person, a place, an object, etc.
Preparation	You will need a collection of pictures.

Procedure

1 Display a number of pictures and then describe one of them, or part of one of them.
2 Invite the learners to identify the picture or detail you have described.
3 Let the first learner to make the identification correctly take over your role.

Variation 1 Someone or something you know

1 Describe anything known to the learners – objects, people, places, sports, etc. which relates to their experience and language level.
2 Ask them to identify what you have described.
3 The learners can then take over your role, describing something well enough for the class or their partner to identify it.

Examples of subjects you might describe
Objects or people in the classroom
Places or buildings in the town
Famous people
Stories or programmes on television

CONNECT: *COMPARE, MATCH, GROUP*

3.6 Bingo

Family	CONNECT: *MATCH*
Language	Listening for chosen words or phrases within a given topic, and reacting as they are heard
	Variation 1 Practising vocabulary by identifying definitions of words
	Variation 2 Listening for rhyming words and practising different phonetic combinations

Preparation	Decide on a group of words that you wish to practise, totalling not more than about 25, and write them on the board. You may choose to practise numbers, for instance: either sequences (e.g. *1–25*) or a selection of numbers which present listening problems (e.g. *13* and *30*, *19* and *90*). Or, instead of numbers, you may wish to use minimal pairs (e.g. *pin/pen, box/books*, etc.). Alternatively, brainstorm with learners on to the board a number of words related to an area of vocabulary you would like to revise.

Procedure

1 Show the learners how to make a *Bingo* grid – a rectangle about 10 cm x 15 cm divided into four parts (or more for older and/or more proficient learners).

2 Tell the learners to write down any four of the items (words or numbers) from the board on to their Bingo grid.

3 Read out the words on the board in any order, making a note of them as you do so. If the learners hear a word that they have written in their Bingo grid they should cross it out. The first learner to cross out all four items on their list calls out *Bingo!*, and reads out the list to prove the claim. This person is the winner.

mouse	sheep
hat	bean

To make the game more challenging, you might want to put each item into a sentence, so that the learners must listen carefully for the words they have chosen, for example, *Brenda lives at 19 Church Street.*

4 If you wish, you could continue until you have read out all the words to enable all the learners to complete their grid and to be able to shout out *Bingo!*

More examples of items you can use in Bingo

Phonetics: For example, you read out *mouth*; they cross out *mouth* but not *mouse*.

Opposites: For example, you read out *big* and they cross out *small*.

Variation 1 Bingo definitions

Preparation | Choose a set of words you would like the learners to revise, for example, clothing, office equipment, food, etc., and write these words on the board. Be prepared to give a definition of each word chosen.

1 Ask the learners to choose and to write down four of the words from the board.
2 Call out definitions of the words in random order. Learners cross out items on their list as they hear the corresponding definitions. For example, if the topic is clothing, and one of the words is *mittens*, you might say: *You wear these outside in the winter to keep your hands warm.* Learners with *mittens* on their list should cross it off.
3 When the learners are familiar with this variation of *Bingo* you can ask them to prepare a topic. They should choose from 10 to 20 words from a topic and write out a definition of each word. In order to ensure that other learners hear correct English, you might like to look at each learner's definitions and to correct them if necessary. The learners then carry out the activity with the rest of the class.

Variation 2 Bingo rhyming words

Preparation | Decide on which phonetic combinations you would like the learners to focus on, for example the sounds /aː/, /ɪ/; /ks/, /ɒ/

1 Introduce the game by writing on the board examples of words containing the sounds you have chosen. Have a different column for each

sound. Invite examples of rhyming words. For example, you might write *box*. Learners may suggest the following rhyming words: *fox, chicken pox, locks, socks, rocks.*

2 Ask the learners to choose and write down four of the words, each word containing a different sound.

3 Read out a list of words, some of which should contain the examples on the board and some not. The first learner to hear and tick off each of his or her four words is the winner. Make sure you keep a record of the words you have read out so that you can check the winner's claim to be the first with all of his or her words crossed out.

Variation 3 Learner Bingo grid

1 Divide the class into groups of four to six. Each group represents a *Bingo* grid. Each learner represents one word.

2 When a learner hears his or her word called, he or she sits down.

Note

For more uses of Bingo see 7.17 **Bingo grammar.**

ORDER

3.7 Most important – least important

Family	ORDER
Language	Writing dictated sentences and ranking them (subjectively or objectively) in order, from most to least important
Preparation	Make a list of five sentences, keeping the learners' interests and concerns in mind. For example, in a business English class, you might want to use quotes from famous business entrepreneurs.

Procedure

1 Dictate five sentences. Tell the learners that they should think about the meaning and decide if they are important, not very important, or totally unimportant. If they are important, the learners should write them at the top of the page; if only slightly important, they should be written in the middle; and if unimportant, at the bottom of the page.

2 Then ask the learners to number each of the sentences they have written in the order of importance for them.

3 Next, tell them to take a different colour pen and number the sentences again according to the order in which they think their neighbour might have placed them.

4 Finally, ask learners to compare their 'guessed order' with their neighbour's 'real order' and discuss the reasons for their choices.

Example

Teachers must know a lot about their subject.
Teachers must help all the students equally.
Teachers must be kind and fair.
Teachers must be very strict.
Teachers must be friendly.

Note

This activity combines all the characteristics of traditional dictation but involves an appreciation of (and response to) meaning. It is a technique that invites a follow-up discussion.

Acknowledgement

We first came across this idea in a Mario Rinvolucri workshop. See *Dictation* by Paul Davis and Mario Rinvolucri, Cambridge University Press 1988.

3.8 Put the story in order

Family	ORDER
Language	Writing a series of sentences dictated in random order, predicting and then determining their correct order
Preparation	You will need a text in which the sentences are in a clear order. Write your own text, or find one, e.g. a joke, a description of an event, etc. Tailor your choice of text to fit with the interests and concerns of the learners. For example, for a business English class, you may want to use 10 stages in developing a selling campaign.

Procedure

1 Dictate the sentences of the chosen text out of sequence.

2 Encourage the learners to predict whether the sentence is from the beginning, the middle or the end of the text, and to write the sentences

correspondingly at the top, in the middle or at the bottom of the page. Then ask them to number each sentence according to the order they think the text is in.

3 Ask the learners to compare their sentence order with that of their neighbour, then reveal the true order.

An example of a story you might like to dictate. Dictate the sentences below out of sequence.

A man in Manchester had a vintage Jaguar car.
It was very old and valuable.
He loved it.
One day he parked it in town and went shopping.
When he returned he found a big dent in one door.
He also found a note under the windscreen wiper.
He read the note.
'Dear owner of the lovely Jaguar. My car hit your car. I am very sorry. I am writing this note because I want people to think that I am giving you my name and address. I am not a fool.'

CREATE

3.9 Visualise and describe

Family	CREATE
Language	Listening to a story for gist and detail
	Responding to the story subjectively, seeing mental pictures, then describing them in writing
Preparation	Choose or write a bare-bones story, i.e. one with very little description.
	You could, if you wish, provide some soft music.

Procedure

1 Read or tell a story to the class, who must sit with their eyes closed and imagine what you are describing. Read quietly, perhaps against a background of quietly playing music.

2 Every so often, stop and ask them to look, listen and feel in their minds for images of what you are describing. Give them two minutes to write down the answer to the question you ask about what they saw or heard or felt. Give each of your questions a number.

3   When the story is finished, ask the learners to work together and to exchange answers to each of your questions. (The numbering will help them to share responses to the same question.)

4   Go through the questions again, inviting comparisons of different perceptions across the class.

5   Later the learners might write up their notes as a story. The stories can be displayed and the class invited to read each story and to vote for the strangest story of all.

Here is an example of a bare bones story with suggested questions below
Close your eyes. Imagine you are in a wood. It is the evening time. ... (1) (2) ... In the wood there is a house – a strange house. ... (3) ... Somebody is coming out of the house. ... (4) (5) ... They are coming towards you. ... (6) (7) ... And now? What happens? ... (8)

You can ask the learners questions about what they saw and you can give them prompt words:
1   *Are the trees big, old trees or young, thin trees? (tall / dead / broken branches / leaves / bushes / grass / stones / rocks / stream, etc.)*
2   *What colour is the sky? Is it dark or light? (sunset / red / orange / purple / clouds / storm / gale / wind / lightning, etc.)*
3   *What is the house like? Is it big or small? What colour is it? (stone / plaster / cracks / hole in the roof / broken chimney / broken windows / dark / lit windows / curtains / door / wood / painted / flower boxes / neat garden / grass / flowers / hens, etc.)*
4   *Who has come out of the house? Is it a man or a woman or a child? Or something else?*
5   *What do they look like? (old man / big man / like a mountain / thin / fat / long hair, etc.)*
6   *How are they coming? Walking or running? Quickly or slowly? Shouting, singing or silent?*
7   *How do they feel? (crying / smiling / laughing / happy / angry / sad / surprised, etc.)*
8   *What happens next? (then / next / suddenly, etc.)*

Notes

- 'Visualisation' is the word commonly used to refer to seeing pictures, diagrams, writing, etc., in the mind.
- A few people cannot see pictures in their minds with any clarity. However, this does not prevent them from writing a description from their general imagination.
- See also 1.11 **Visualisation.**

4 Mainly writing

There are different reasons for writing in the foreign language classroom:

- We can see, very readily, the learners' proficiency level: what language items the learners can use correctly and what mistakes they make. This is the traditional and still useful role for writing.
- Many who are visual learners need to write in order to engage their way of learning ... they need to *see* the language. Writing with this purpose means that it is relevant even for learners who take no written examinations.
- Learners can be made aware of the many different purposes for writing in society: describing, narrating, advising, etc.

Writing, like speaking, is normally intended to communicate something to somebody. It is thus an advantage if writing activities in the classroom result in someone reading the texts that the learners write *and then responding to them in an appropriate way*, rather than just you, the teacher, marking the texts for errors of form. If there is a response from a reader, then the writer finds out if the reader was engaged, was able to follow the ideas, and was able to appreciate the points made in the text. You can then help the writer to reflect on his or her communicative success, or lack of success, deriving from the form, i.e. the choice of words and the arrangement of them. In this way form can be related to communication.

The games in this section assume this close relationship between form and communicative purpose.

IDENTIFY: *DISCRIMINATE, GUESS, SPECULATE*

4.1 True and false essays

Family	IDENTIFY: *DISCRIMINATE*
Language	Recognising or attempting to work out the definitions of words and to distinguish true definitions from false ones
	Using a dictionary to find the definitions of words
	Using a wide range of language to write plausible false definitions for real (and possibly imaginary) words

Procedure

1 Ask each learner to write an essay based on descriptions of real places and/or events, and tell them that each essay must contain five things that are not true.
2 Invite each learner to read at least three essays, and try to find the five untrue bits of information in each one.
3 If it proves difficult to find the five untrue bits of information in a particular essay, then invite the writer to read it to the whole class, and try to find the five things together.

Variation 1 True and false sentences

1 Organise the class into pairs. Ask each pair to write ten statements on separate strips of paper, some true and some false.
2 Invite the pairs to exchange their strips of paper and try to group them into true and untrue statements.

Variation 2 True and false dictation

1 Organise the class into pairs. Ask each pair to write five sentences, some which are true and some which are not.
2 Invite the pairs to take turns dictating their sentences to the rest of the class, who should write them down and decide which are true and which are not.

Variation 3 True and false definitions

Preparation	Find a word unfamiliar to the learners, a definition of it, and a sentence exemplifying its meaning and use, as well as two or three false but plausible definitions and exemplifying sentences for the same word. Provide dictionaries for the learners.

1 Read all your definitions and sentences to the class, and ask the learners to decide which one they think is correct.
2 Once a decision has been reached, or the learners agree to differ, tell them to consult their dictionaries and check for themselves.
3 Once the class is accustomed to the game, ask individual learners to prepare one true and two or three false definitions of words as well as exemplifying sentences for the rest of the class. This could well be done for homework. Alternatively, ask groups of learners to do this preparation cooperatively.
4 To add complexity and fun, permit the mixing-in of an *imaginary* word, complete with definition and exemplifying sentence, into the series of genuine words.

DESCRIBE

4.2 Draw the bank robbers

Family	DESCRIBE
Language	Defining the appearance of a person in writing using descriptive language
	Reacting to written descriptions of physical appearance by drawing the characters described
Preparation	Provide a copy of a description of a fictional bank robber for each pair of learners. When inventing your bank robber, you may want to draw a picture of him/her before writing the description, but do not show the picture to the learners.

Procedure

1 Tell the learners to write *WANTED* at the top of a piece of A4 paper.
2 Ask the learners to study your description of the bank robber and to make a large drawing of him or her on the poster. (Don't let the learners see your drawing of the robber, if you did one.) Here is an example of the kind of description you might provide:

> *He has got a very small head.*
> *His head is the shape of a pear.*
> *His right ear is as big as a plate.*
> *His left ear is small and like a cup.*
> *His left eye is very small and his right eye is very wide.*
> *His left eyebrow is longer than his right eyebrow and it is nearer to his eye.*
> *His eyebrows are very bushy like hairy caterpillars.*

3   Display all the drawings and discuss those that do not tally with the description. Help the learners to appreciate the need for precision.

4   Invite pairs to invent a bank robber of their own and write a description of him or her, guided by your description of your robber. Set a time limit for this.

5   Ask each pair to exchange their description with another pair, who try to make an accurate drawing of the person described.

6   Tell each pair to pass the new drawing to yet another pair of learners, who write a description of the person based on the drawing.

7   Ask pairs to give this second description to one last pair, who must try to make an accurate drawing of the person described.

8   Invite learners to display and compare the sets of drawings and texts.

Variation 1   Describe from memory

Preparation   Find four pictures of people who look somewhat similar.

1   Show the four pictures all at once to the whole class. Tell the learners to decide which picture they want to describe, and not to let anyone else know their choice. Give them a short period of time, e.g. 10 seconds, to look closely at it, and then (from memory) to write a description of it.

2   Encourage the learners to mill around, asking three other learners, in turn, to read their description. They should then try to identify which picture has been described.

Variation 2   Describe an object

1   Brainstorm a list of objects on to the board.

2   Ask each learner to write a description of one of the objects.

3   Tell the learners to mill around, asking at least three other learners to read their text and to see if they can identify which object has been described.

Examples of language items the learners might find useful

It's red/green/brown with white spots. (colour)
It's big / small / very small / smaller than a bottle top. (size)
It's round / square / long. (shape)
It's made of wood / metal / rubber / plastic. (substance)
It's used for eating / fighting / working / feeding dogs. (purpose)
It belongs to Harry / an old man / a young woman. (owner)

Note

Even beginners can write descriptions by listing single words or short phrases, for example *Green. Write. Draw. Teacher.* (These four words describe a chalkboard.) Or: *It is a rectangle. It is made of wood and it is painted white. It has a handle and a lock.* (A door.)

More advanced descriptions might proceed along the following lines: *People may like an object or a situation or other person, but sometimes they may have a much stronger feeling. Sometimes this strong feeling is positive in its effect and sometimes negative.* (Love.)

Examples of other 'describe-and-do' activities

Learner A describes a fantasy animal. Learner B draws it.

Learner A describes a route through a town. Learner B draws a street map plus features which are important in finding the way.

Learner A describes a journey through the countryside. Learner B draws the route and the things which can be seen.

Learner A describes his or her room. Learner B draws an exact plan and location of each object.

Learner A describes a scene and a simple series of actions. Learner B represents the scene and actions with three-dimensional objects, e.g. a box representing a house, an eraser representing a person, and then carries out the actions.

Learner A describes an event or film or an institution or abstract concept and Learner B identifies it.

CREATE

4.3 Bouncing dialogue

Family	CREATE
Language	Writing dialogue using role play and a wide range of language

Procedure

1 Ask learners to work in pairs to create a dialogue between two characters. For example, one learner can be a parent, the other a teenage child, and the situation is that the teenager was given permission to come home at midnight, but came home at two o'clock in the morning.

2 Tell the learners that they must not speak, but only read silently and write in response as they bounce the dialogue to and fro between them.

Example of a dialogue between father and son
The first line written by Learner 1, acting as the father, might be:
Father: *So there you are!*
And Learner 2, acting as the son, might respond:
Son: *Dad! I can explain!*
Father: *OK! I always enjoy your explanations!*
Son: *But Dad! It really wasn't my fault. I was …*
            etc.

---

3 Finally, ask volunteers to act out their dialogue to the whole class.

Other ideas for bouncing dialogues
Parent and teenage child discussing:
        Raising pocket money
        Bad behaviour reports from school
        Bullying
Famous people discussing:
        What it is like to be famous
Fictional characters discussing:
        The differences between their experiences and points of view
The learners as themselves discussing:
        Learning English
        What they would like to be doing if they were not in school
        A totally fictional exciting experience
The learners adopting names and characters and chatting as if on the Internet.

Notes

- You can add to the amount of work done by asking each pair to bounce two different dialogues between each other at the same time.
- You could use MSN Messenger or Skype on the Internet so that your learners can actually chat to each other on the Internet.

4.4 Bouncing stories

Family	CREATE
Language	Writing a story collaboratively, using a wide range of language
Preparation	(optional) Display three pictures on the classroom wall.

Procedure

Invite learners to get into pairs and silently bounce two stories between them, each one adding a sentence to the text passed to them by their partner.
   Here are some conditions you might like to specify.

1   You determine the amount of time allowed for reading the text already written and adding a sentence to it by ringing a bell and insisting that the text bounce back immediately, even if the sentence is only half written, in which case it must be continued by the partner.
2   You insist on all the stories relating to three pictures that you display on the board. The stories will all be different in detail, but will all be related in theme through their relation to the same pictures.
3   Instead of adding a *sentence*, you can specify that the learners are only allowed to add a *single word* to the story before passing it back again.
4   Instead of bouncing between two learners, the text can bounce along a line of learners, for example, all passing the text they have initiated to their right, at the same time. It should go through about eight people, who each add a line and pass the paper to their right, before finally being returned to the learner who wrote the initial sentence.

4.5 Bouncing letters

Family	CREATE
Language	Writing creative letters using role play
Preparation	You will need one card per learner, two normal-sized envelopes per learner (optional), and a box or other container to hold the cards. Either leave the cards blank and have the learners prepare them as explained below, or – to save time and keep up the tempo of the game – write the name of a different famous person or fictional character on each one.

Procedure

1   Brainstorm the names of famous people (e.g. *Julius Caesar*) and/or famous fictional characters (e.g. *Mickey Mouse*) with the learners. Give

a small blank card to each learner as they suggest a name and ask them to write it on the card. Continue in this way until there is one completed card per learner. Put the cards in a box (or bag or hat).

2   Ask each learner to take a name card at random from the box to represent their new identity. Tell them to keep it secret!

3   Put the cards back in the box, then ask each learner to take a card once again.

4   Tell the learners to assume their 'secret identity' and write a letter – in character – to the person named on the second card they took. You might like to specify the theme of the letter, for example, asking to borrow something, and set a time limit for letter-writing, for example, ten minutes.

You may need to give the learners a format for writing letters, a structure for their letter and other support, for example, useful phrases, according to their proficiency level.

Examples of a letter structure and some useful phrases to write on the board
Introduce yourself: name, job, etc:
> *May I introduce myself. My name is ...*

Say what you need and why it is important for you:
> *I want to ... but it is very difficult because I haven't got a ...*
> *If I can't ... then ... might happen.*

Ask if they have it and if you can borrow it:
> *May I ask if you have a ...? May I borrow it?*

Say how long you want it for:
> *I would like to borrow it for ... days/months/years.*

Say how you will reward them:
> *If you lend it to me, then I will be very grateful and I would like to ...*

---

5   Ask for volunteer letter carriers. Give them the letters and ask them to find the people they are addressed to. For example:
> Letter carrier: (calling out the name on the letter) *Julius Caesar!*
> Julius Caesar: *Here!*

6   Let the learners open and read their letters.

7   Tell the learners to write back to the sender of the letter. If the theme of the letter was a request to borrow something, then learners should say *either* that the sender may borrow the object requested and what the

conditions will be *or* that the sender may not borrow the object and the reasons why not.

8   Ask the letter carriers to deliver these answering letters.

9   Let everyone open and read their letters, then invite some learners to read out both the letter they wrote and the letter they received.

10   Display all the letters in pairs.

11   Finally, bind all the letters together in a book.

Example of a letter from Julius Caesar to Mickey Mouse

The palace
Rome

Dear Mickey,
Please can you help me? Brutus and the others want to kill me. I am sure they do. They think I want to be Emperor, but I don't. Who wants to be Emperor? Do you? May I borrow your cat-proof vest until the end of March? I will wear the vest under my toga. Nobody will know. I will give it back to you in April.
If you lend me your vest, then I will export all the cats in Rome to Egypt. They like cats there.
Best wishes,
Julius
P.S. Please, give my love to Minnie!

Note

This is an opportunity to discuss the relatively formal style of the traditional letter in comparison with the informality of e-mail exchanges. We learned this game from Michael Beaumont.

4.6 Ambiguous picture story

Family	CREATE
Language	Speculating as to the subject of an ambiguous picture, using expressions of uncertainty, e.g. *It could be … It might be … It looks like …* *If the line is a road then the square could be a house.* Writing a story inspired by an ambiguous picture, using a wide range of language
Preparation	Find, or draw, an ambiguous picture similar to that on the next page.

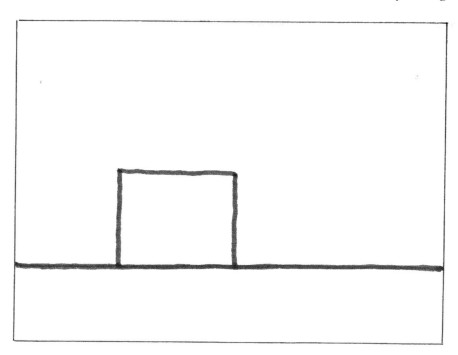

Procedure

1 Begin by asking the learners to say what they can see in the picture.

Learner 1: *I think there is a flat field and there is a square house on it.*

Learner 2: *No! It's a box in a room.*

Learner 3: *It isn't! It's a square hole in a wall.*

2 Take one of the interpretations and use questions to establish a story.

Teacher: *If it's a box in a room, then tell me about the room. Is it a big room or a little room?*

Learner 1: *It's a little room.*

Learner 2: *It's in the cellar of the house and there is no window.*

Learner 3: *It's dark.*

Through questions, help the learners to establish the beginning of the story.

3 Then ask each learner to write the story beginning made by the class, but to finish the story in his or her own way.

4 Invite the learners to mill about and read their finished stories to several other learners. Their reading might make them want to modify what they have written.

5   Finally, collect all of the stories and publish them as a book, putting the ambiguous picture on the cover. Give the book a title, for example, *The Mysterious Box. A collection of stories by ....*

4.7 Rewrite a fairy story

Family	CREATE
Language	Rewriting a well known fairy story in a humorous, creative way

Procedure

1   Ask the learners to rewrite a well-known fairy tale and to be as funny as they can possibly be. Here is an example based on *Little Red Riding Hood*:

> *Little Red set off on her motorbike and went to the Pizza Max where she bought an extra large 'Four seasons' pizza for her grandmother. She bought an extra large pizza because she liked pizzas herself.*

Set a time limit, but allow learners to finish their stories later, perhaps for homework.

2   Encourage each learner to read his or her story to at least three other learners in turn.

3   Display all the stories and have the class vote for the silliest one.

4.8 Story consequences

Family	CREATE
Language	Writing parts of a text, guided by cues as to general purpose, but deprived of the ability to communicate with or see the contributions of one's co-authors

Procedure

1   Divide the class into groups of eight players. If you have smaller groups then some of the learners must write two sentences or more.

2   Demonstrate how to fold a piece of A4 paper into eight strips: fold the paper in half, then in half again, and in half one last time; making all the folds parallel. Then, guided by the resulting creases, refold the paper into zigzags, like the squeezy parts of a concertina or accordion. Ask one learner from each group to fold a piece of paper in the same way.

3   Explain that the game proceeds as follows. The first player writes their
     contribution on the first panel of the concertina, i.e. the topmost panel.
     The player should do this quietly and secretly, folding the panel over
     when they are done, so that no one else can see what was written. Next,
     the second player follows suit, then the third, and so on, until all eight
     contributions have been added. The last player has the task of unfolding
     the concertina and reading out loud to the others the full text of the little
     story that results.

     The story is guided by the following formula, which prescribes what
     each player should contribute:

Fold 1   (time) …
Fold 2   (place) …
Fold 3   X (male character's name) *met …*
Fold 4   Y (female character's name)
Fold 5   *He said …*
Fold 6   *She said …*
Fold 7   *The consequence was …*
Fold 8   *and …*

Example

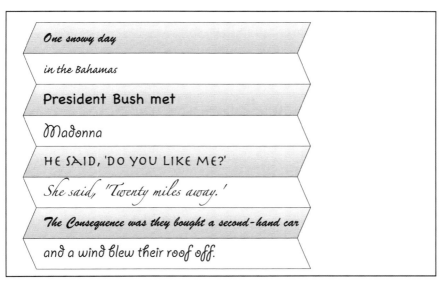

Variation 1   New Year's resolutions

In many countries it is customary, on New Year's Day, to promise improved behaviour for the following year. The idea of the 'New Year's Resolution' provides a basis for a variation of the above *Story consequences* game.

1   Divide the class into groups of five learners.
2   Ask each group to make a four-part concertina (see main game) and add to it in turns.

Fold 1   *I*, (name), *will* ...
Fold 2   (resolution),
Fold 3   *if* (name) *says he/she will* ...
Fold 4   (resolution).

---

3   Invite the fifth learner to read the complete text to the class.

Example

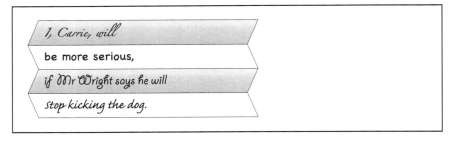

I, Carrie, will

be more serious,

if Mr Wright says he will

stop kicking the dog.

4.9   Five-line poem

Family	CREATE
Language	Writing a five-line poem on any subject, guided by instructions as to the parts of speech (e.g. noun, adjective, verb, adverb) and figures of speech (e.g. simile) to be included in each line

Procedure

Challenge the learners to write a five-line poem in which the first line is a noun, the second is two adjectives (joined by *and*) which describe the noun, the third is a verb and an adverb to describe the noun in action, the fourth begins with *like* and presents a comparison, and the fifth starts with *if only* and expresses a wish.

Here is an example by Sven Grüner, a Norwegian student:

> noun ....*Politician*
> adjective + adjective .... *phony and false*
> verb + adverb ....*lying desperately*
> like ....*like a mocking bird*
> if only ....*if only I had the key to the bird cage*

4.10 What's in his pocket?

Family
Language

CREATE
Tracing somebody's movements over a number of days, and writing a report explaining the motivations behind their comings and goings, based purely on physical evidence

Expressing oneself in writing using varying degrees of certainty

Preparation Make a collection of *any* objects which could be carried in someone's pockets, particularly objects collected on a journey or on an evening out.

Provide a small collection of these objects *or* photocopies of objects for each group of about 6 learners. (Alternatively the whole class could work from the same objects.)

Here is an example of a collection made at the end of a journey overseas:

1 Air ticket Manchester–Copenhagen–Oslo.
2 Travel agency receipt.
3 Various exchange slips from banks.
4 A small brown paper bag from China.
5 An envelope addressed to Norway with the stamp torn off.
6 A postcard of the mermaid in Copenhagen, stamped but unused.
7 A list of 16 strangely assorted objects.
8 A scrap of paper with 'petrol £25' written on it.
9 Two tickets for an art gallery.
10 A beer mat with a name and number on it.

You may wish to ask the learners to help you to make a collection of such objects.

Procedure

1 Either divide the class into groups and give each group a collection of objects (see above) or let the whole class work from the same collection of objects. Invite the learners to behave like detectives examining physical

evidence. They should try to find out who the objects belong to, who the person is, what their interests are, where they have been, what they have done, whom they have met, etc.

2 Ask the learners to prepare a full written account of what they have deduced about the identity and comings and goings of the owner of the objects, being sure to back up their claims with references to the pieces of evidence.

Example of a written statement based on various objects

Mr A. Wright, who lives at 12 Bielfeeld Road, Manchester, M2 0BH, bought an air ticket from Delta Travel Agency, Manchester, on 12 July. The ticket was for a flight from Manchester to Oslo via Copenhagen. While he was in Norway he met someone who had been to China (the bag appears to be genuinely from China) ... etc.

---

3 If all groups refer to the same objects, the written accounts may be compared and displayed.

Note

If you use objects from a situation or journey you were on, or are familiar with, then the aim can be for the learners to hypothesise a description that is as near to the truth as possible.

4.11 Speaking to the world

Family	CREATE
Language	Using a wide range of language to write a short speech

Procedure

1 Tell the learners: *You are the first person to arrive on Venus.* The whole planet Earth is waiting to see you and to hear what you say live on TV. Your government has given you a statement to read but you can say something of your own, too. You have twenty-five words before the censors cut you off. (You might like to change this so that the statement is for the inhabitants of Venus to hear.)

2 Encourage the learners to write, read out and display what they would say.

3 Have the class vote for the funniest, the most serious, and the most moving speeches.

4.12 Create an island

Family	CREATE
Language	Creating a map of a fantasy island, guided by questions with a focus on geography (directions, distances, lakes, rivers, mountains, etc.) Writing a travel journal describing travels and adventures using a wide range of language Adapting the travel journal into a story form Working collaboratively
Preparation	You will need a large sheet of paper (A1 or A2).

Procedure

1 Invite the learners to create a fantasy island on the board and help them by guiding them with statements and instructions. For example:

> Teacher: *Draw an island on the board. Draw it as big as you can. North is at the top. South is at the bottom. West is on the left. East is on the right.*
> *How long is your island?*
> *Are there any mountains or hills on your island? Where are they?*
> *So the mountains are in the north of the island. And they are about five kilometres across. How high are they?*
> *Has your island got any rivers? Where does the river begin and where does it finish?*
> *Has your island got any lakes/marshes/forests?*
> *Are there any villages/castles or other special places on your island?*

2 Once the island is created on the board, copy it on to a large piece of paper (A1 or A2), so it can be displayed for all the class to see, and can be re-used in future lessons, and ask the learners to copy the map into their notebooks.

3 Introduce the idea of adventures on the island. Begin by saying that you are the captain of a ship that is going to put them on shore and come back for them in a week (or more, if you wish the game to last longer). They must try to survive during that time. Discuss and agree with them what provisions and tools they should take with them.

4 Ask the learners to form groups of two or three, in which they will continue the adventure. Tell them that they will keep a travel journal in which they make entries including the date and time, as

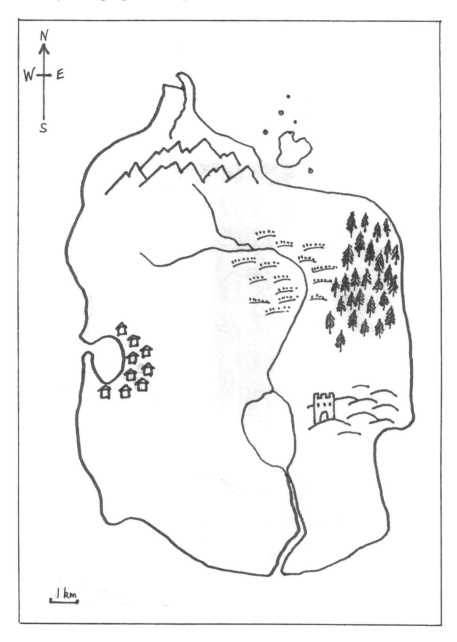

well as notes about what they see, hear, say, feel, and the situations which occur.

5 When their journey is over, after a week (or whatever other duration you chose at the beginning of the game), have the learners write their full story and draw a map to show their exact route. Display their maps and stories. Learners might even want to display their notes, adding to the sense of adventure and intrigue by singeing the paper, tearing it, dropping stains on it, or letting it suddenly stop in mid sentence to show that the journey ended prematurely for these unfortunate travellers.

Notes

- The potential of the created island is considerable. The map can be used again and again in reference and in full activities over the following months.
- Details can be added, perhaps on separate paper: caves, buildings, sources of danger or fun or food, etc. Residents can be introduced and their characters and concerns built up over the months.
- Such an island becomes an important part of the learners' lives and a source of increasing creativity and a reason for writing as well as for reading, speaking, listening and cooperating as a class.

4.13 Create a soap opera

Family	CREATE
Language	Using as wide a range of language as possible to continuously or periodically create and share a core of characters and episodes in their lives, guided by questions, photos, and the creative contributions of other learners
Preparation	Choose two photos of people as the starting point; as the 'series' progresses, you or the learners may wish to introduce other materials. For younger learners you may prefer to choose two soft toys.

Procedure

1 Discuss with the learners what they know about soap operas: titles, names of characters, the personality of the characters, etc. Tell the learners that they will be creating a soap opera.

2 Show the learners the two photos of people that you have selected, and tell them that these are the central characters. Ask questions to establish an identity, personality and concerns about each of them according to the learners' language level and level of sophistication. Encourage the

learners' inclination to make the characters serious portrayals of real people or to create fantasy people. It is better not to imitate an existing soap opera.

Emphasise that they must come to a consensus and may not arbitrarily change the information about the characters. Any changes that do occur must be brought about through the forces of experience in the lives of the characters. In order to develop a feeling for character and the influence of character on the development of the story, you might like to suggest that the learners think of a few aspects of the personality, appearance and abilities for each character.

Examples of character identity
A character can be created based on age, sex, job, family, friends, pets, hobbies, food/music preferences, etc.

Further characteristics might be added: aspects of the character's personality and behaviour, concerns, successes, frustrations, use of language.

Examples of further character detail
She is very pretty but not intelligent.
He wants people to think that he is intelligent, but he isn't.
She is very warm, friendly and helpful.
He is a bully and he is dangerous.
She is jolly and always singing.
He can't stop stealing things.
She is very ambitious.
He is very lazy.
She works very hard.
He lives in his dreams.
She likes animals more than people.

---

3 Ask the learners to find pictures (or, in some cases, real objects) for homework which illustrate different aspects of the protagonists' lives, for example, a car, a house, a holiday, etc. Discuss and agree on the appropriate information about these aspects according to the learners' language level.

4 Display these photographs and real objects together with the pictures of the characters. Write on a poster what the class has agreed about each aspect. This will act as a guiding model for the learners when they invent their own person.

5   The learners make a copy of this poster in their Soap Opera books. They can represent the two protagonists by their names.

Example of the first few lines of description
His name is Henry Coconut.
He is 25 years old.
He lives with his mother.

Example of later descriptions
He pretends that he is confident, but really he is always worried.
He can't sleep at nights. He has nightmares. He is frightened of all animals and birds.

---

6   Extend the community by asking each pair or group of learners to create another protagonist, to choose a picture of him or her, and to write down his or her particulars, then introduce their character to the rest of the class. Discuss how the new characters might relate to the central protagonists. This must be in their Soap Opera book.
7   The learners can then walk about in the class holding the picture of their character in front of them and pretending to be that character. They meet other characters, exchange names and ask for other information and decide whether they want to be friends or not with each of the others.
8   After this activity the learners can make a relationship diagram and write a description of the relationships. They can also write a letter to

some of the others, telling them about their meeting and why it was important to them. Copies must be kept in their Soap Opera books.

9   Discuss and agree on a place for these people to live. It might be a city district, or a small town or a village. It might be on an island. Decide where each person lives. Draw plans and maps, find or draw pictures, etc. and record these in the Soap Opera book.

10   Introduce an event, for example, *the electricity supply for the town breaks down.* Help the learners explore what the different people do, how they interact, what stories they have to tell. You can help by asking questions about where the characters were, how they were affected, what they thought, felt, said and did, etc. Ask the learners to write articles about the event for the local newspaper. Again, record everything in the Soap Opera book.

11   Decide, with the learners, what will happen next, based on your teaching programme and in accordance with the living drama the class has created.

These are some of the topics you might introduce
Creating ...
a village, town or city district for the community (the topography, flora and fauna, industry, history, etc.)
relationships in the community: families, friends, enemies
dramatic events affecting the characters, e.g. natural disaster and its effect (flooding, epidemic)
differences in the community about issues, which can be real, contemporary issues, e.g. young and old generations in conflict about modernising versus preserving traditions

---

Examples of ways of using writing in a class soap opera
Creating a book of the characters, places and events
Sending letters from one character to another
Writing a community newspaper
Designing posters, invitations, graffiti
Writing a book of ghost stories set in the community
Writing a history of the community and area
Writing dialogues for particular events in preparation for video or audio recording
Writing a journal about the characters and events
Creating a real website for this fictitious community

Notes

- The procedure given here is one of the many ways in which a fictitious community can be established and the dramas created. Please note that in this game the learners are not primarily actors but *creators* of the characters and the dramas. However, there is no reason why parts of these dramas cannot be extracted and produced as video soap opera episodes.
- This game offers a wonderful opportunity to recycle language and to introduce new language items. It also offers a natural context for all skills including writing and reading (letters, e-mails, websites, newspapers, party invitations, etc.). It can be played at any language level.
- Because the learners create the community and the drama, they can blend realism and fantasy in any way they wish.
- Because they are creating together, there is an enormous feeling of good will.
- Many learners are familiar with this idea through computer games which allow the players to create characters and places and to create dramas with them.
- You, as the teacher, might like to use such an idea only occasionally or you might like to make it a complete alternative to the course textbook … or somewhere in between!

5 Mainly reading

We normally read in order to get information that is relevant to us. Our practical reading skills are sponsored and developed by this aim. The games in this section involve the learners in looking for and responding to meaning rather than responding to a text in a formal way.

The games call for a *manifested response*, that is to say, a response in which the learners do something to communicate to others their understanding, their feelings and their ideas, rather than just a response that is private.

Two important skills are concentrated on, namely *skimming* for gist, when the learners find out at speed what content a text contains, and *scanning*, when they search a text for some particular item in it.

DO: *MOVE, MIME, DRAW, OBEY*

5.1 What's my mime?

Family	DO: *MIME*
Language	Showing understanding of a text by miming it
	Skimming and scanning a series of texts to find one corresponding to actions being mimed
	Scanning a text for a particular language point
	(optional) Writing texts that focus on actions (with special attention to verbs and possibly combinations of verb tenses)
Preparation	Display on the board a list of sentences that express actions which could be mimed. Alternatively, give a photocopy of the list to each learner.
	The sentences could be written by the learners, or you could write them yourself. When writing or choosing sentences, you may wish to favour ones that not only offer practice in skimming and scanning, but also allow revision of a particular language point.

Procedure
1 Reveal or distribute the list of sentences to the learners.
2 Invite learners to take it in turns to mime any sentence on the list. Encourage the learners watching the mime to try to identify what is being mimed and then scan the list to find which sentence is referred to.

Examples of simple actions

A man is walking.
A woman is swimming.
A boy is playing football.
A girl finds some money on the ground.

Examples of more complex actions

A waiter was carrying many plates of food on both arms when he fell over a child.
An old man was reading a book when he heard his mobile phone and he looked for it in his pocket.
A young woman was walking along the road when she saw a friend on the opposite pavement.

Notes

- This game can also be played in pairs.
- There is a musical chairs version of this game, where learners walk around a line of chairs (one chair for each person) listening to music. One chair is removed and then the music stops and all the learners try to sit down. The one learner who cannot sit down not only loses his seat, but must also mime one of the sentences before being out of the game.

IDENTIFY: *DISCRIMINATE, GUESS, SPECULATE*

5.2 Telepathy (texts)

Family	IDENTIFY: *GUESS*
Language	**Main game** Creating and concentrating on mental imagery in response to texts skimmed for gist
	Attempting to 'read' the imagery in another learner's mind
	Variation 1 Skimming texts for gist in order to find the most

	important one, then to determine which one might be the most important to each of a number of other learners
Preparation	You will need four or five short texts. Good sources are: proverbs, wise sayings, headlines, brief quotations, points from a set of notes, lines from a poem, principles, etc. Either display these on the wall or board or provide a photocopy for each learner.

Procedure

1   Say that you intend to carry out an experiment to test telepathic communication. If you (as we, the authors,) do not believe in telepathy, then say so to the class.

home from home
home sweet home
home truth
close to home
home and dry

2   Display the texts you have chosen and ask for a volunteer. Tell the volunteer to choose one of the texts, picture it in their mind, and concentrate on it as hard as they can, in an attempt to transmit telepathically to the rest of the class which text they are thinking of.

3   Invite the rest of the class, whether they believe in telepathy or not, to try to guess which text was chosen. Each learner should write down the text they have guessed. Allow two minutes for this part of the game.

4   After two minutes, ask the learners to read out their chosen text, in turn. (In this game it is remarkable how everyone *wants* to listen to everyone else. Everyone wants to be right!) You may prefer to give each text a number and to ask the learners to refer to the text they chose by number.

5   Ask someone to stand by the board and to keep track of the number of votes for each text.

6   When the votes have been counted, ask the volunteer to say which text he or she was thinking of. Decide together whether the learners were successful in mind reading! Discuss whether the experiment proved or disproved the possibility of telepathy.

Note

This game can also be played to practise the present continuous – see 7.5
Telepathy (pictures).

Variation 1   Guess the preferences of others

1   Display the five texts you have chosen and ask each of the learners to
    decide which one they think is the most important.
2   Ask each learner to try to guess which text each of the other learners in
    their group might have chosen, based in this case on empathetic
    understanding, not on an attempt to read their minds.
3   Let the learners check their predictions, then find out who made the most
    correct predictions.

5.3   Flashing a text

Family	IDENTIFY: *GUESS*
Language	Predicting the contents of a text based on brief glances at its contents, indications as to its general meaning, as well as familiarity with word order and the habitual grouping of certain words
Preparation	Display a short text on an OHP transparency, on the board, or on a large piece of paper.

Procedure

1   Flash your chosen text at great speed, especially the first few times you
    reveal it. This makes the game challenging. For example, if you are using
    an OHP, swing a book between the projector and the screen, giving the
    learners only a split second's view of the text between swings. Flash the
    text as many times as you feel is fun and effective.
2   Encourage the learners to guess at what has been seen, and make no
    comment about whether it is correct or not. The learners do not have to
    try to read the text word by word, but may call out any part of the text
    that they have seen. Slowly build up the complete text with them. To
    make the game easier you may tell them the topic of the text.

Don't put all your eggs in one basket.

5.4 Texts word by word

Family	IDENTIFY: *SPECULATE*
Language	Speculating about the meaning, contents, source, nature and purpose of a partially hidden text
Preparation	You will need a short text, for example the start of a children's story, a letter, a holiday brochure.

Procedure

1 Reveal a text word by word. You can show it on the overhead projector, or write it word by word on the board, or you might like to have the words on cards and to prop them, one by one, on the shelf at the bottom of the board.

2 As you progressively reveal the text, ask questions about the possible meanings of each word exposed and its relationship with the words already revealed. Also ask questions to encourage the learners to speculate about the origin and purpose of the text.

Examples of questions you might ask as the text is revealed
What does the word mean?
What sort of word is it? (noun, verb, article, etc.)
What word(s) might come next?

Examples of questions you might ask when some or all of the text has been revealed
What is the source of the text? Is it from a magazine, a publicity leaflet, a children's book, a travel book, a financial institution statement, a tombstone?
Who wrote it?
What kind of readers is the text written for?
How does the writer want to affect the reader?

Notes

• You may like to write the questions about the whole text on the board and to ask the learners to work together in pairs on their answers.

• If you use cards, you can place a mark on the top of the card to represent the position of the word within the sentence.

CONNECT: *COMPARE, MATCH, GROUP*

5.5 Pelmanism (reading)

Family	CONNECT: *MATCH*
Language	Skimming for gist in order to match pairs of cards
Preparation	Make a set of 10 pairs of cards for each group of three to four players. Alternatively, ask the learners to make the cards themselves. The latter is both time-saving for you and more involving for the learners.
	The pairs of cards can relate to each other in a range of ways, according to the language needs of the learners. (See below for examples of different types of matching pairs.)

Examples of text pairs
word / definition
quotation / author
photo (from a magazine) of a person, object or scene / a written description of him/her/it
photographs / matching dialogue
cartoon / caption (cut from comics, etc.)
riddle / solution
question / answer
action / purpose

Procedure

1   Invite the learners to form groups of three or four. Give each group a set of cards, and help them become familiar with the pairs. A simple way to do this is to invite them to muddle all the cards face up and then see how quickly they can pair them together.

2   Ask the learners to shuffle the cards and lay them *face down* so that the pictures and/or writing on the cards cannot be seen. It doesn't matter if the players see the cards being put down and if they try to remember where the pairs were placed.

3   The first players in all the pairs then pick up two of the cards. If they think their cards match, they make some appropriate comment to the others, before picking them up. For example (if playing with word / definition cards):

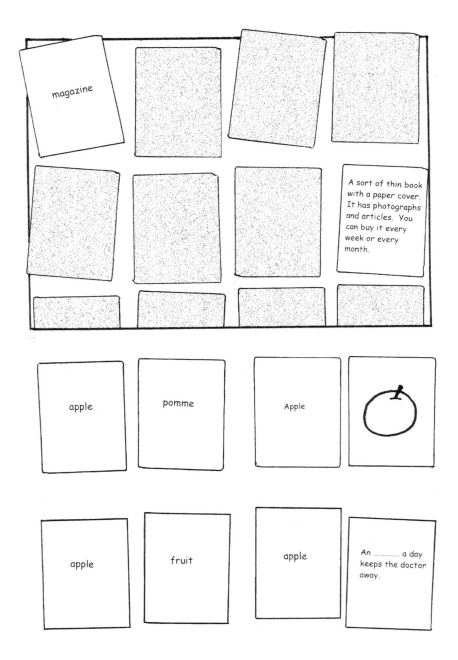

magazine

A sort of thin book with a paper cover. It has photographs and articles. You can buy it every week or every month.

apple

pomme

Apple

apple

fruit

apple

An .... a day keeps the doctor away.

Player 1:   (pointing to the back of a card) *Magazine!* (turns over the picture … if it is a picture of a magazine then they leave it turned over)

(pointing to the back of another card) *A sort of thin book with a paper cover. It has photographs and articles. You can buy it every week or every month.* (turns over the card … if the picture and the text make a pair, the player leaves them turned over)

4   If the others agree that the cards are a pair, the player keeps them and takes another turn.

5   When two cards are picked up which do not match, they must be shown to the other players and replaced in exactly the same position from which they were taken. Then the next player has a turn.

6   This continues until all the cards have been paired off. The player with the most pairs is the winner.

ORDER

5.6 Jumbled texts

Family	ORDER
Language	Cooperatively sequencing pieces of a jumbled text, first skimming for meaning to establish a quick order, then scanning for detail to confirm its accuracy
Preparation	You will need a short text cut into pieces and reproduced enough times for each group of learners to have a copy; one complete copy of the text for the teacher; an envelope for each jumbled copy of the text.

When choosing and cutting up your text, keep the following in mind:

1   Your text may be an article, a story, a joke, a poem, a letter, an essay, an argument, etc.

2   You may wish to cut the text into paragraphs, verses, sentences or even half sentences.

3   Interest is added if you choose illustrated texts.

4   The game can be graded in difficulty by (a) the text you choose; (b) the number of pieces you cut the text into; (c) the degree to which pictures (if there are any) help to give the meaning of the text.

Procedure

1   Divide the class into groups of about four learners. Give one envelope of jumbled text components to each group, then ask the learners to read each of the pieces and place them in the correct sequence.
2   Ask the groups to tell you when they are ready, so you can check that their sequence is correct. The first group to finish with a correct sequence is the winner.

Note

You can make the game more challenging by mixing two or more texts.

Variation 1 Stand in order

Preparation	Take a short text and cut it into as many pieces as there are learners. Keep a copy of the complete text for yourself.

1   Give one piece of the text to each learner.
2   Invite the learners to walk about in the classroom, reading out the words in their own piece of the text, and listening to those of their fellow learners. Ask them to arrange themselves in a line or a circle according to the sequence in which they think their pieces appear in the text.
3   When they are ready, ask the learners, in turn, to read out their piece of text.

5.7 Proverbs

Family	ORDER
Language	Ordering or ranking sentences according to personal importance, perceived value, etc. Predicting a fellow learner's order Explaining the reasons for one's choice of order
Preparation	Make a list of ten proverbs, wise sayings or statements on large pieces of paper to display on the board. Provide ten strips of paper for each learner.

Procedure

1   Give each learner ten strips of paper.
2   Put ten proverbs, wise sayings or statements on strips of paper on the board. Ensure that they are understood.

3   Ask the learners to copy the sentences on to their strips of paper, then to rank them into the order of importance for them. Alternatively, you may ask the learners to divide the statements into three groups, for example, *most important, fairly important* and *not so important*.

   If you identify each sentence by a letter, A, B, C, etc. then the learners can very easily keep a note of their decisions about rank order.

4   Then invite each learner to guess the order in which their neighbour has ranked the proverbs.

5   Ask learners to compare their results and discuss the differences with their neighbours. Encourage them to discuss the reasons motivating their choice of order or ranking.

Examples of proverbs
Actions speak louder than words.
Art is long and life is short.
A barking dog never bites.
Better safe than sorry.
A bird in the hand is worth two in the bush.
Boys will be boys.
Curiosity killed the cat.
Every cloud has a silver lining.
Don't count your chickens before they are hatched.
Don't cry over spilt milk.
Don't put all your eggs in one basket.
The grass is always greener on the other side of the fence.
A hungry man is an angry man.
The leopard does not change its spots.
Don't cross your bridges until you get to them.
It's never too late to learn.
You cannot have your cake and eat it.

Examples of wise thoughts
Only the educated are free.
Education is the ability to listen to almost anything without losing your temper or your self-confidence.
By nature all people are alike, but by education widely different.
Children have to be educated, but they have also to be left to educate themselves.

Knowledge is power.
Information is thin stuff, unless mixed with experience.
The great difficulty in education is to get experience out of ideas.
We trust our heart too much, and we don't trust our head enough.
To be able to enjoy one's past life is to live twice.

You might play this game using statements from topics such as:
Foods (preferences, dietary value)
Friendship (characteristics)
Social behaviour (characteristics)
School rules
Advice to young people
Personal objects (car, mobile phone, etc.)

You could also use:
Quotations (quality of advice, humour)
Extracts of poems

REMEMBER

5.8 Running dictation

Family	REMEMBER
Language	Memorising and dictating a text
	Recording a dictated text accurately in writing
Preparation	You will need a text printed on paper.

This wonderful game derives from the classic resource book, *Dictation*, by Paul Davis and Mario Rinvolucri, Cambridge University Press 1988.

Procedure
1 Depending on the size of the class, display one or more copies of the text on the classroom wall or on a table.
2 Divide the learners into pairs and have each pair decide who will be Learner A and who will be Learner B.
3 Explain the rules of the game as follows: Learner A must run to the text, read it, and try to memorise as much of it as possible before running back

to Learner B. Learner A should then dictate what they remember of the text to Learner B, who should record it in writing. Learner A can run to the text as often as is necessary to complete dictating the whole text.

4 Applaud the first pair to finish with no mistakes.

5.9 Memorise and draw

Family	REMEMBER
Language	Skimming a description of an image, scanning it for detail, then memorising it in order to draw the most accurate replica possible
Preparation	You will need a picture or a map and a written description of it. (See an example on the next page.)
	Display the description on the wall so that learners can go and consult it. Keep the picture or map hidden from sight until the end of the game.
	Note The written descriptions might be prepared by the learners themselves. In an earlier lesson or homework you can ask them to write a description of the picture or map that you intend using in this game. Correct their descriptions and ask the learners to rewrite them. Choose one for use in the game.
	Alternatively, you may prepare the text yourself.

Procedure

1 Invite the learners to leave their desks and read the description posted on the wall, skimming at first, for the general idea, then scanning for detail and memorising the essential points of the description.

2 Ask the learners to return to their desks and draw a picture of what has been described. Let them return to re-read the description as often as they need.

3 Display all the pictures and discuss which relate well to the text and which less well.

4 Finally, show the original picture or map upon which the description was based. Ask the learners whose picture or map is the most accurate replica.

Notes

• The text can be an objective description of a person, place or object, so that an accurate replica of the original might be expected, or the description might be subjective, in which case the learner can respond subjectively.

Can You Draw It?

There is a road across the middle of the map. The road
is called King's Road.
There is a crossroads half way along King's Road. The
other road is called Queen's Road.
'Prince's Road' is about 100 metres up Queen's Road
on the right.
John's house is about 200 metres on the left on Prince's
Road.

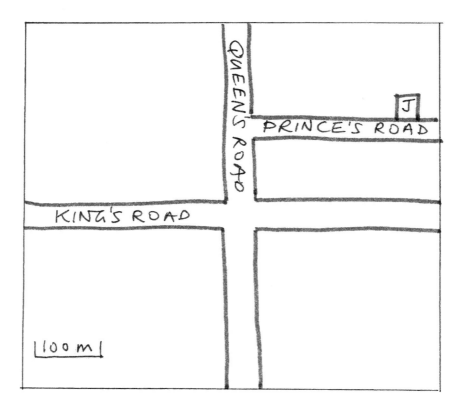

- If you collect all the corrected descriptions and then hand them out again randomly, every learner will have his or her text responded to and will get the feedback of the drawing as evidence of the success of his or her description.

5.10 Pass the message

Family	REMEMBER
Language	Reading a short text seen for a very brief time and writing it down as accurately as possible from memory
Preparation	Write a short message on a slip of paper, for example one of the following:

1 *Please phone me this evening.*
2 *Don't forget to empty the washing machine, feed the cat and lock the door.*
3 *I will be waiting for you just outside the swing doors of the swimming pool at a quarter to nine.*

You might first consider discussing the prevalent and destructive nature of rumour with the class. Then introduce this game as an example of how easily words and meanings can be confused and corrupted.

Procedure

1 Show the message to someone sitting at the front and to one side of the class. Let this learner see the sentence for five seconds, then take it from them and keep it.

2 Ask that learner to write the sentence as they remember it on a piece of paper, and to show it to their neighbour for five seconds.

3 Carry on with your normal lesson as the message is passed from learner to learner, each learner writing down the message they remember. The message, usually much changed, should eventually reach the last learner.

4 When the message has been passed through all the learners, ask the last one to read out what they have written down. There will probably be cries of astonishment!

5 Then read out the message as it began.

6 Now ask all the learners, in turn, to read out the message *they* passed on.

7 If you want to get some intensive language work out of this game, particularly for advanced students, discuss why each of the changes might have occurred. Are they changes which don't change the sense significantly? Are the changes due simply to grammar mistakes? Making a detailed analysis of these changes can be a very subtle and informative activity.

6 Mainly vocabulary and spelling

We can communicate with vocabulary more readily than with grammar. Extending the learners' vocabulary is important, right from the earliest stages.

Learning vocabulary must be based on attaching meaning to the word, rather than just remembering the form of the word. Meaning can be brought to the new word through translation, but our aim in this section is to help the learners *experience* the meanings of the words in context by using them for *purposes which matter to them.*

Occasionally, it may be necessary to draw attention to the form of a word *as well as* its meaning, and a few games in this section do that, for example, 6.2 I Spy and 6.10 Hangman spelling.

IDENTIFY: *DISCRIMINATE, GUESS, SPECULATE*

6.1 Feely game

Family	IDENTIFY: *GUESS, SPECULATE*
Language	Asking questions, and naming objects: *What is it? It's a …* Expressing uncertainty: *I don't know. It could be a …* *I'm not sure. I think it's a …* *I know what it is, but I don't know what it's called.* *I know what it's called in (Swedish), but I don't know what it's called in English.* **Variation 1** Describing objects and speculating about them **Variation 2** Asking questions about objects and their owners **Variation 3** Speaking whole sentences, e.g. lines from a song, and identifying the speakers **Variations 4–9** As in main game
Preparation	You will need about ten small objects of different shapes and sizes and a piece of cloth, a thin towel, or a headscarf, which must be large enough to cover four or five of the objects. For pair work, you should provide enough objects and pieces of cloth, etc., to keep all the learners occupied.

If the objects are very different, then it is not really a challenge to identify them by touch, so choose some which are similar to feel, e.g. pens/pencils, coins of different denominations, plastic bags/paper bags, screws/nails.

(optional) You could provide some pairs of gloves, to make feeling more of a challenge.

Note Instead of a covering cloth, you may choose to conceal the objects for touching in a box or bag.

Procedure

1 Make sure that the learners know the names of the majority of the objects which you have collected.

2 Put four or five of the objects under the cloth on a table without the class seeing which ones you have chosen.

3 Ask a learner to feel one of the objects through the cloth and to tell you what they think it is. Let the learner remove the object to see if they were correct.

4 Repeat with other learners.

Notes

- The language in this game can be restricted to:

  Teacher: *What is it?*
  Learner: *It's a …*

  Alternatively, the language of uncertainty might be used (see the information box above).

- If you think that the learners, divided into pairs, can collect a sufficient number of objects, you will find the game easy to arrange for pair work.

- To make the game more challenging, do not show the objects beforehand. You might also make the 'feeler' wear gloves!

Variation 1   Touch and describe

Ask more advanced learners to talk about each feature of the object they are feeling in such a way that the rest of the class can identify it. This will require the use of descriptive terms and the language of speculation, for example:

Learner 1:   (feeling the object) *It's hard.*
Learner 2:   *What's it made of?*
Learner 1:   *I think it's made of plastic.*
Learner 3:   *What shape is it?*
Learner 1:   *It's long and rectangular.*

Learner 4:   *Is it a ruler?*
Learner 1:   *Yes.*

Variation 2 Identify an object and its owner

Preparation	You will need a scarf, or other blindfold, and a collection of objects, as above.

1   One learner is blindfolded and sits in the centre of a circle. One of the other learners places an object (or objects) in his or her hands, and asks:
       Learner: *What is it / are they?*
                        Who does it / do they belong to?
    That is to say, the blindfolded person must identify both the object(s) and the owner.
2   If this is done correctly, the two players change places. If not, another object, belonging to a third person, is placed in the first person's hands, and the game goes on as before.

Variation 3 Identify by listening to a voice

Preparation	You will need a scarf, or other blindfold.

1   Blindfold a learner.
2   Ask another learner to come forward and stand quietly next to the blindfolded learner and say something to him or her, for example, an English proverb, or a quotation from a song, rhyme or textbook being studied by the class.
       Teacher: *Who's this?*
       Learner 1: *To be or not to be, that is the question.*
       Learner 2: (blindfolded and listening to the voice) *Eva?*
       Learner 1: *No, listen, again. To be or not to be, that is the question ...*
       Learner 2: *Julia!*
       Teacher: *Yes.*

Variation 4 Identify by listening to an object

Preparation	As above, provide a collection of objects. For classwork, erect a barrier or screen of some kind on your desk, for example, a cardboard folder, to prevent the class from seeing what it is that you are doing. For pair work, provide a barrier – books work well – or blindfold for every second person.

1   Drop an object behind the barrier and encourage learners to guess what it
    is.

> Teacher: (dropping a pencil sharpener behind the barrier) *What's*
> *this?*
> Learner 1:   *A pen.*
> Learner 2:   *No, it's a pencil sharpener.*
> Teacher: *Yes, well done.*

2   Repeat with different objects.
3   Move into pair work, if the pairs can get enough objects ready to drop.

> Learner 1:   (dropping an object behind the barrier on to the desk)
> *What's this?*
> Learner 2:   *A key.*
> Learner 1:   (dropping the same object again) *No, it isn't.*
> Learner 2:   *A coin.*
> Learner 1:   *Yes.*

If appropriate, encourage learners to use the language of uncertainty (see
information box above).

Variation 5   Identify by smelling

Preparation	Provide a blindfold and a collection of objects, all with distinctive smells, e.g. *coffee, tea, bread, cheese, chocolate, apple…*

Blindfold a learner and invite him or her to identify something by smell.

> Teacher: (holding the substance near the learner's nose) *What's this?*
> Learner 1:   *I think it's …*

Variation 6   Identify by tasting

Preparation	Provide a blindfold, a collection of objects, all with distinctive tastes, and spoons for feeding the foods to the learners. Check that none of the objects is unsuitable for use with the learners, whether for reasons of health (allergies), or for reasons of diet (vegetarian, halal, etc.), and, in the interest of hygiene, use a clean spoon for each learner.

Blindfold a learner and invite him or her to identify something by taste.

> Teacher: (feeding the learner with a spoon) *What's this?*
> Learner 1:   *I think it's …*

Variation 7 Identify by looking

Preparation	Choose a picture with details which the learners can identify and name, for example, a footballer, or an animal, or a distinctive building.

1 Pull the picture slowly out of an envelope, or reveal it bit by bit from behind a book, starting from the top.
2 Keep asking the learners what they can see. Get them to speculate. Encourage different opinions. There is then a reason for listening and speaking.

> Teacher: *What is it?*
> Learner 1: *It's a head.*
> Learner 2: *Hair.*
> Teacher: *Is it a man or a woman?*
> Learner 3: *A man.*

Variation 8 Building up a picture

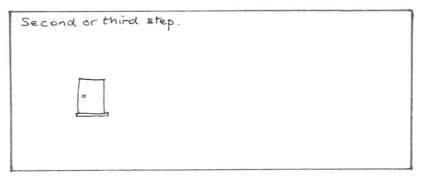

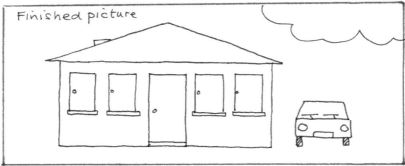

Progressively draw (or have a learner progressively draw) the parts of a picture, all the while inviting guesses as to what is being drawn.

Teacher: (draws a dot on the board) *What is it?/ What do you think it is?*

Learner 1: *It's a dot. It's an eye.*

(Teacher adds another element to the picture.)

Learner 2: *It could be a door.*

(Teacher adds another element.)

Learner 3: *It's a window.*

Teacher: *And what's this and this?*

Learner 4: *Another window... and a door... It's a house.*

Variation 9 Strip of a magazine picture

Preparation	Cut off a strip of a magazine picture, about 5 mm or 1 cm wide and as long as you like. Choose a picture which contains on the strip fragments of several objects, all of which the learners can name. Glue the strip on to a card which is slightly wider than the picture strip. Draw arrows aiming at all the fragment of objects, and give each arrow a number. Write the names of the objects on the reverse of the card.

1 Ask the learners to try to guess what each numbered part of the strip is.
2 Tell the learners to check their guesses with what you have written on the reverse of the card.
3 Once the learners have seen how to do this, you can ask them to make a magazine strip of their own, and give it to you for others to play with. There is an example on the next page.

Note

Select the pictures that you use for this game according to the topic and vocabulary area you want the learners to practise.

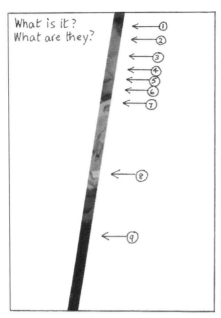 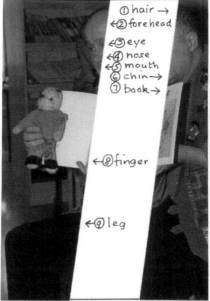

6.2 I spy

Family	IDENTIFY: *GUESS*
Language	Vocabulary for objects in the room

Procedure

1 Begin by choosing an object to refer to in the classroom and then say, *I spy with my little eye something beginning with* ... (the initial letter of the word for the object you have chosen). Explain, if necessary, that *I spy* means *I can see.*

2 Invite the learners to try to guess what it is.

    Teacher: *I spy with my little eye something beginning with B.*
    Learner 1: *Book?*
    Teacher: *No.*
    Learner 2: *Board?*
    Teacher: *Yes.*

3 The winner takes over your role.

    Learner 2: *I spy with my little eye something beginning with* ...

Note

You could widen the scope of this game by asking learners to imagine that they are somewhere else, for example, *Imagine that we are in a supermarket. I spy with my little eye something beginning with ...*

6.3 Silent speaking

Family	IDENTIFY: *DISCRIMINATE*
Language	Any area of vocabulary, focussing specifically on pronunciation of limited sets of words, for example, colours, numbers, animals, minimal pairs
Preparation	Choose a topic you would like the learners to practise.

Procedure

1 Brainstorm on to the board words related to the topic you have chosen.
2 Select one of the words and speak it silently to the class, moving your mouth as if speaking it, but not making any sound.
3 Ask the class to identify the word.
4 Have the learners take turns doing the same thing with a partner.

6.4 Stories in ten words

Family	IDENTIFY: *GUESS*
Language	Using and recognising key words from any story or topic This may be objective when everybody agrees, or subjective when a personal explanation is necessary. It can be left as a vocabulary activity or lead to discussion.
Preparation	Choose a well-known story, e.g. *Little Red Riding Hood*.

Procedure

1 Ask the learners to guess the name of a familiar story by listing key words and phrases for them. For example:

　Teacher: 　*I am going to tell you a story. Tell me what the story is.*
　　　　　　Girl, mother, grandmother, basket, forest, wolf.
　Learner 1: *Little Red Riding Hood.*

2 Ask learners to repeat this activity in pairs. One learner lists five to ten key words from a familiar story, and the other identifies the story. Then they switch roles.

Note

Re-telling a story, using key words, is a good way of building confidence. The learners feel they have achieved something by identifiably representing an extended text. As a basic technique, in the earlier years, the volunteering of single words naturally leads to the volunteering of longer phrases and eventually of complete sentences.

Variation 1 Key words in a topic

Preparation	Prepare (mentally or on paper) a list of topics which you would like to practise, e.g. work, school, holidays, food, college or school, home, sports, hobbies, animals, seasons.

1 Write several topics on the board, for example: *school, food, holidays, hobbies*.

2 Ask learners to copy the words from the board and to write at least three words they associate with each topic. The teacher can say whether the three words should be general associations or personal associations. For example, we might all agree that *school* can be associated with *teacher, classroom* and *chalkboard*, but we may not all associate *school* with *worry, bullying, noise, friends* and *games*.

3 Each learner shows their collection of associated words to at least one other person who must try to guess which topic is referred to. Or, instead of showing their three words to other individuals, learners can display their words on a notice board so that others can read them and decide which topic or story they describe.

    Learner 1: (has written *turkey, cookies, oranges, walnuts*)
    Learner 2: *Is the topic food?*
    Learner 1: *No.*
    Learner 2: *Is it holidays?*
    Learner 1: *Yes.*

Note

This is a good way into the discussion of a topic area.

Variation 2 Word webs

1 Demonstrate, on the board, how to make a word web centring on a topic, shown by a word or short phrase. The web of associated words can be general associations or personal associations.

2   Brainstorming with the learners, make a list of about 20 topics on the board.
3   Ask each learner to choose three topics from the list and make webs of words they associate with each one, being careful not to identify the topic on their word webs. In other words, the central circle should be left empty.
4   Tell the learners to circulate, showing their webs to at least three other learners, who must try to identify the topic of each web.

Example of a general word web for car

Example of a personal word web for car

6.5 Mime and guess

Family	IDENTIFY: *GUESS*
Language	**Main game** Adjectives that apply to people
	Variation Adverbs
Preparation	Decide what type of adjectives you would like to revise.

Procedure

1   Tell the learners what type of adjectives you will be reviewing. Help them brainstorm a list of five to fifteen adjectives and write them on the board. Here are some examples of adjectives describing feelings: *surprised, bored, miserable, busy, frightened, angry.*
2   To play this game as a class activity, ask one learner to mime an adjective. The rest of the learners should try to guess what he or she is miming. Alternatively, divide the class into two teams.

1 Write one of the adjectives on a piece of paper and hand it to one player from the first team.
2 That player must mime the word and his or her team should try to guess it within a set time limit (say, two minutes). If they guess right, the team wins a point. For example:

Mimer: (mimes action)
Learner 1: *Are you tired?*
Mimer: (shakes head, continues miming)
Learner 2: *Are you lazy?*
Mimer: (shakes head, continues miming)
Learner 3: *Are you bored?*
Mimer: *Yes!*

3 You could then encourage the other learners to find the reason for his/her boredom. For example:

Learner 4: *Are you bored because you have nothing to do?*

4 Next it is Team 2's turn.

Variation 1 Mime an adverb

1 Help learners brainstorm a list of five to fifteen adverbs and write them on the board.
2 Tell one learner to choose an adverb that will be easy to demonstrate, no matter what action he or she is asked to do. The choice should be kept secret.
3 Encourage the class to propose actions that the learner should perform in the manner of his or her chosen adverb. If nobody can guess the word, then the class can give one or two more actions to mime expressing the same adverb. For example, the mimer may have chosen *angrily*.

Class: *Open and close the door.*
Mimer: (opens and closes door angrily)
Class: *Noisily!*
Mimer: (shakes head)
Class: *Walk to the teacher's desk.*
Mimer: (walks angrily)
Class: *Quickly!*
Mimer: (shakes head)

You might insist that learners' guesses combine the adverb with a verb in a complete sentence. For example *Are you opening and closing the door noisily?*

6.6 Draw a picture / Guess what I'm drawing

Family	IDENTIFY: *GUESS*
Language	Vocabulary from any chosen area
Preparation	Decide what area of vocabulary you want to practise, e.g. verbs, adjectives, animals, etc.
	Write words from the chosen area on small cards and drop them into a bag or a box for the learners to choose from.

Procedure

1   Divide the class into teams of about seven or eight.
2   Ask one learner from one team to take a word card and to draw on the board what is on the card in no more than ten seconds.
3   Allow the artist's team to call out what they think the drawing represents.
4   Award points accordingly. If they are correct on their first try, the artist's team gets three points; if they are correct on their second try, they get two points; on their third try, one point. You must be the referee. If the called-out word is not exactly the same as the word on the card you might still decide to award the points.
5   If the artist's team fails to guess the word after three attempts, give the other team a try and award them with one point if they guess correctly.

Notes

•   The game is easier if you tell the class which topic they are dealing with, for example, animals.
•   You may decide to allow the use of miming after the drawing has been done.

CONNECT: *COMPARE, MATCH, GROUP*

6.7 Word associations

Family	CONNECT
Language	General vocabulary
	Asking for and giving reasons, using *Why ...?* and *Because ...*

Procedure

Each learner, in turn, says a word he or she associates with the word given by the preceding learner. This should be done as a fast game. Sometimes you or another learner may interrupt and ask why a word was chosen. For example:

Learner 1:	*Water.*
Learner 2:	*Tap.*
Learner 3:	*Kitchen.*
Learner 4:	*Grandma.*
Teacher:	*Why did you say 'grandma'?*
Learner 4:	*Because I thought of my grandma's kitchen.*
Teacher:	*OK. Grandma.*
Learner 5:	*Wolf.*
Learner 6:	*Why did you say 'wolf'?*
Learner 5:	*Because of the story of Little Red Riding Hood.*

Note

You might like the learners to use a formula, such as *When I hear 'water', I think of 'tap'.*

Variation 1 Personal lists

1   Ask the learners to brainstorm a list of ten words and write them on the board. You can use any words at all, but here is an example: *desk, paper, clock, lunch, dog, cat, happy, tired, homework, music.*

2   Ask each learner to put the words into sequence according to how they feel one word is associated with another. It is a good idea to set a time limit for this part of the activity.

3   Ask one learner to begin to read out the words on his or her list and explain the connections between each item.

> Learner 1:   *I am **tired**. I look at the **clock**. I am **happy**, because the English class is almost over. After English I have **lunch**. I will eat a hot **dog**.*

6.8 Odd-one-out

Family	CONNECT: *GROUP*
Language	Almost any vocabulary area, for example, colours, family relations, animals, household utensils
	More demanding examples include: extracts from poems, names of famous people, countries, etc.
	Asking for and giving reasons, using *Why ...?* and *Because ...*
	Starting a discussion

Preparation	Prepare 10–15 groups of words, each of which contains an 'odd-one-out', for example:

a) *horse, cow, mouse, **knife**, fish*
b) *David, Michael, Andrew, **Alison**, Adrian*
c) ***plate**, bean, soup, sandwich, apple*
d) ***bicycle**, bus, car, motorcycle, lorry*
e) *green, **big**, orange, brown, red*
f) *brother, father, **sister**, uncle, grandfather*
g) *June, January, March, **Spring**, May*
h) *Rhine, Danube, Po, **Hudson**, Thames*
i) *Shakespeare, Milton, J. B. Priestley, **Laurence Olivier***
j) *Paris, Ottawa, **New York**, London*

Present the words to the learners on the board, on an OHP or on paper.

Procedure

1 Tell the learners to identify the word from the first group that they think is the 'odd-one-out'.

2 Ask individuals to say which word they chose as the 'odd-one-out' and to say why.

3 The other learners should be asked if they agree; or, if they disagree, to say why. You should not say which answer you think is correct until this discussion is finished – partly because this would inhibit discussion and partly because there may be no *one* correct answer.

4 Each of the groups of words can be discussed in turn in this way.

Notes

• The words used should, of course, reflect the interests of the learners, and could be from a topic of a specialist nature from sport to business to engineering.

• Once learners are familiar with this game, they can be asked to compile their own sets of words, each containing one they consider to be the 'odd-one-out'. These sets can then be used in classwork.

Variation 1 They're all odd!

Instead of looking for the single word which doesn't fit with the others (as in the main game, above), ask the learners to explain why each word can be seen as the 'odd-one-out'.

> mouse, fish, knife, horse, cow
>
> Mouse is the odd-one-out because it is the only one which is not useful to people.
>
> Fish is the odd-one-out because it is the only one which swims in the sea.
>
> Knife is the odd-one-out because it is the only one which is not a creature.
>
> Horse is the odd-one-out because it is the only one which carries people.
>
> Cow is the odd-one-out because it is the only one which is called cow!

Variation 2 Somebody must go!

Preparation Make a list of six or eight interesting characters – they may be known *public figures* such as politicians, rock stars or actresses, *fictional characters* from fairy tales or television programmes, *members of different professions* such as teachers, comedians or lawyers, etc. The list should include about six or eight characters. Present the list on the board or on an OHP.

1   Present the list to the learners, and explain that these characters are on a life raft that is overloaded and sinking. Two of the six (or three of the eight) must be thrown overboard in order for the others to survive.
2   Have each learner suggest who should be sacrificed and why. Encourage debate and discussion about the relative importance and usefulness of each character, and the ethics underpinning the whole game.
3   You may want to take a vote at the end of the discussion to determine which characters remain on the life raft.

6.9 Vocabulary cards

Family CONNECT: *MATCH*
Language Vocabulary from any area
Preparation Make a set of 10 pairs of cards for each pair of learners. Alternatively, get the learners to make the cards themselves. The latter is both time-saving for you and more involving for the learners.

The pairs of cards can relate to each other in a range of ways, according to the language needs of the learners. (See below for examples of different types of matching pairs.)

Examples of matching pairs

mother tongue word / English word

gapped sentence / missing word

word / picture

word / definition (e.g. *grape / a small, round, purple or green fruit that you can eat or make into wine*)

British English word / American English word (e.g. *boot / trunk*)

opposite word / opposite word (e.g. *big / small*)

Topic-based pairs

animal / the food it eats (e.g. *sheep / grass*)

animal / a country it lives in (e.g. *elephant / India*)

sport / an object which is typical of the sport (e.g. *golf / club*)

map of a country (from travel brochures) / the name of the country

photo of coin or stamp / the name of its country of origin

pictures of different fish, trees, birds, flowers, etc. / their name

Collocations

adjective / noun (e.g. *fatal / accident*)

verb / noun (e.g. *play / football*)

verb / adverb (e.g. *listen / carefully*)

object / characteristic (e.g. *gold necklace / valuable*)

object / category (e.g. *table / furniture*)

tool / job (e.g. *saw / carpenter*)

capital / country (e.g. *Canberra / Australia*)

synonym / synonym (e.g. *big / large*)

suffix / root (e.g. *–ful / care*)

digit / number (e.g. *7 / seven*)

rhyming word / rhyming word (e.g. *heart / part*)

phonetic pairs: long and short vowels (e.g. *beat / bit*)

phonemic script / word (e.g. teɪbl / *table*)

Procedure

1 Give each individual or pair of learners the same set of cards and have them start to match the pairs of cards at the same time.

2 As learners finish they call out *Finished!*

3 Tell the learners to check their matchings against the answer sheet.

Note

This game is a good one for making the learners familiar with the cards and preparing them for Variation 1.

Variation 1 Pelmanism or remembering pairs

1 Divide the class into groups of three or four.

2 The learners lay the cards, in neat rows, *face down* so that the pictures and writing on the cards cannot be seen. The pictures must not be put in pairs, but randomly placed. It doesn't matter if the players see the pictures being put down and if they try to remember where the pairs were placed.

3 The first player then turns over two of the cards, one at a time. If the player thinks the cards match, he or she should make some appropriate comment to the others before picking them up, for example:

> Player 1: (pointing to the back of a picture) *Apple!*
> (turns over the picture … if it *is* the picture of the apple, then he or she leaves it turned over)
> (pointing to the back of another picture) *Apple!*
> (turns over the picture … if it is the second picture of an apple, then he or she has made a pair and can keep it)

4 If the other players agree that the cards are a pair, the first player keeps them and it is the next player's turn.

5 When two cards are picked up which do not match, they must be shown to the other players and replaced in exactly the same position from which they were taken. Then the next player has a turn.

6 This continues until the cards have been paired off. The player with the most pairs is the winner.

To use this game to practise grammar and syntax, see **7.16 Pelmanism (grammar)**; to use it to practise reading see **5.5 Pelmanism (reading)**.

Variation 2 Asking other learners

1 Give one card to each learner.

2 Invite the learners to look at their cards and to try to find who has the matching card by talking to their classmates. For example:

> Learner 1: *I've got a picture of the Canadian flag. What have you got?*

ORDER

6.10 Hangman spelling

Family	ORDER
Language	**Main game** Spelling a word
	Variation Focussing on letter order and placement in words of a fixed length (e.g. five-letter words)

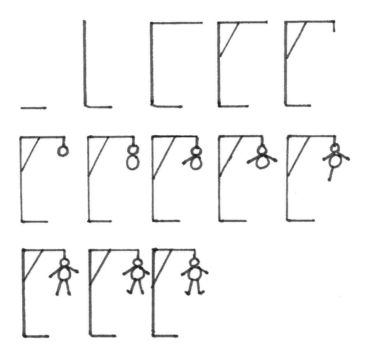

Procedure

1 Think of a word that should be familiar to the learners, and draw a dash for each letter.
2 Invite the learners to call out letters which they think may be in the word.
3 If a learner guesses correctly, write the letter above the appropriate dash. For each incorrect guess, draw one part of the 'hanged man' as in the illustration.

   Teacher: (chooses the word *HAPPY*, draws 5 dashes on the board)

Learner 1: *Is there an E?*

Teacher: *No, there isn't.* (draws one part of the hanged man)

Learner 2: *Is there a P?*

Teacher: *Yes, there are two Ps!* (writes them in above the third and fourth dashes)

4 The game proceeds in this manner either until the learners guess the word, or until thirteen mistakes have been made, the drawing has been completed, and the learners have been 'hanged'. You may then reveal the answer.

Notes

- You may wish to have the learners play Hangman in pairs, instead of as a class.
- Thirteen is thought to be an unlucky number. In pre-Hellenic times the king, who only ruled for a year, was sacrificed in the thirteenth month. There was a thirteen-month year at that time.
- You may not want to use a game based on capital punishment! Instead of the drawing of the hanged man you might prefer to draw 12 dashes on the board and to add the letters to each dash as a mistake is made: *I AM THE WINNER*. Alternatively, you may prefer to have 13 dashes and to write the words: *NEXT TIME LUCKY*.

Variation 1 Words with letters in common

1 Think of a word of a certain length, a five-letter word, for example, and draw the same number of dashes on the board.
2 The learners call out words of the same length. If any of these words contain a letter which is in the word you are thinking of *and* is in the same position, write the letter on the board, over the appropriate dash. For example, you are thinking of *MOUTH*, and a learner calls out *TEACH*. The letter H is in both words, and is in the same position, so you write:

— — — — H

Although the letter T is in both *TEACH* and *MOUTH*, it is *not* in the same position, so you do not write the T.
3 You might like to write each word on the board as it is called out.

REMEMBER

6.11 A long and growing list

Family	REMEMBER
Language	Vocabulary for objects which can be bought
	a and *an*
	Can also be adapted to practise many areas of vocabulary and grammar, including the following:
	adjectives and adjectival phrases
	adjectives in alphabetical order
	nouns and adjectives starting with the same letter
	possession (*have/has got*)
	animals
	simple past
	past continuous
Preparation	Select several sentence patterns suitable for using with vocabulary items that are to be revised. You might also want learners to have their dictionaries or textbooks.

Procedure

1   Play in groups of four to six players, with the players sitting in a circle.

2   Tell the learners that, in this game, a given sentence pattern – *I went shopping and I bought …* – must be completed by adding any words that make sense, each player adding one word to the list when it is their turn. Each player must repeat verbatim whatever has been said by the previous player before making an addition to the list. For example:

Learner 1:   *I went shopping and I bought **a shirt**.*

Learner 2:   *I went shopping and I bought a shirt and **a skirt**.*

Learner 3:   *I went shopping and I bought a shirt, a skirt and **a sausage**.*

Learner 4:   *I went shopping and I bought a shirt, a skirt, a sausage and **an apple**.*

Learner 5:   *I went shopping and I bought a shirt, a skirt, a sausage, an apple and **a car**.*

3   Also explain that each player must act out or mime, however cursorily, each of the items referred to, while speaking. The rest of the class (or group, if the game is based on group organisation) might also mime at the same time. Encourage creative and humorous ideas!

Notes

- This game may be played using other sentence patterns which allow
  learners to focus on different types of vocabulary and grammar points,
  for example:

  The teacher's cat is very old, rather fat, bald with a long beard... (any
  adjectives and adjectival phrases)

  *The teacher's cat is an active cat and a bad cat and a cute
  cat...* (adjectives in alphabetical order plus *a/an*)

  This morning I bought a brown bag ... (noun and adjective with the
  same initial letter)

  *Kirsty has got an elephant, Tom has got a monkey, David has got a
  python, and I've got an armadillo ...* (*has got / I've got* plus animals
  and *a/an*)

  *This morning, before six o'clock, I swam across the lake, and I read
  Shakespeare, and I argued with my neighbour, and I ...* (simple past
  tense)

  *Yesterday, while I was brushing my teeth, I heard a dog singing, and I
  saw the butcher slapping his goldfish, and I thought about my friend
  dancing ...* (past continuous interrupted by simple past)

  Whatever sentence pattern you choose, the challenge of this game is to
  remember and repeat all the additions given earlier and then to
  contribute your own addition. The object of all the variations of the game
  is to see how long and elaborate a sentence learners can devise.

- You might judge that your learners cannot do such a game spontaneously
  and will need preparation time, perhaps in groups, using dictionaries or
  textbooks as necessary. In some of the alternative sentence patterns and
  stipulated rules it might be essential for this preparation to be done, and,
  in any case, preparation then involves everybody.

6.12 Kim's memory game

Family	REMEMBER	
Language	**Main game**	Vocabulary for any objects, or objects in pictures
	Variation 1	Numbers and plurals
	Variation 2	Adjectives and comparisons
	Variation 3	Vocabulary for containers
	Variation 4	Past tenses
	Variation 5	Detailed written description

Preparation	Assemble a collection of small objects or pictures of objects which you know the learners can name. Here are some of the alternative ways of getting a collection together: – a number (nine to twelve) of small objects on a table – a number of small magazine pictures of objects on a table – a number of small, quick sketches of objects on the board or OHP Have a cloth or piece of paper to hide the objects or pictures. If you are using the OHP, you do not need to switch the machine off, since you can simply cover the lens with your hand or a book.

Kim is the hero of the book *Kim*, written by Rudyard Kipling. Kim was trained to be observant, for example by being asked to remember exactly what was on a tray before it was covered up.

Procedure

1 Lay the objects and/or pictures on the table, or display the pictures on the board. Tell the learners that you are going to challenge their powers of observation and memory.
2 Give the learners 20 seconds to look at the objects and/or pictures, then hide them with a cloth or sheet of paper.
3 Tell the learners to write down as many objects (i.e. nouns) as they can remember. Then ask them to tell you what they have written.

> Teacher: *What have you written?*
> Learner 1:   *There was an apple.*
> Teacher: *Good. What else can you remember?*
> Learner 2:   *There was a paper clip and a pen.*
> Teacher: *There was a paper clip, but are you sure there was a pen?*
> Learner 3:   *It was a pencil!*

4 Finally, remove the cloth or sheet of paper and let the learners compare their lists with the objects and/or pictures.

Variation 1 Numbers and plural forms

Preparation	Assemble a group of objects, as above, only be sure to include several which are the same, for example pictures of four suitcases, three cameras and two CD players.

Give learners practice in numbers and plural forms by asking them to write how many of each type of object they saw. The total number of all objects must be enough for it to be a challenge.

Variation 2 Adjectives and comparisons

Preparation	Same as in the main game, above, but you should include several objects and/or pictures which are of the same kind but are of different colour, size, shape, etc.

1 Encourage the learners to use adjectives to describe what they saw in the picture, for example, *a red, a black and a green suitcase.*
2 Tell students to use comparatives to describe the objects seen in a more detailed manner, for example, *The green case is a bit bigger than the black case and it's about the same size as the red case.*

Variation 3 Containers

Preparation	Same as in the main game, above, but restrict your choice of objects to containers of various types, e.g. a bottle of milk, a box of matches, a tin of soup, a packet of soap powder, a bag of apples, a tube of toothpaste.

The procedure is the same as in the main game, with the focus on containers.

Teacher:	*What can you remember?*
Learner 1:	*There was a tin.*
Teacher:	*What was in the tin?*
Learner 1:	*I'm not sure. Maybe it was tomato juice.*
Learner 2:	*No, it was a tin of tomato soup!*

Variation 4 Actions in the past

Preparation	Find a short video or DVD clip (no more than three minutes long) which contains a variety of actions. Advertisements, for instance, often present a large number of actions compressed into a very short time. (The clip doesn't have to be in English, as you can view it with the sound off.)

1 Show the video to the learners, telling them to pay special attention to the actions that occur. Do not let them take notes during the video!
2 Ask the learners to try to remember what happened or was happening or was going to happen and in what order these actions occurred. They may take notes at this point. You may want the learners to work in pairs and see which pair can accurately recall the most actions.
3 Let the learners share their observations with the class.
4 Watch the video again so learners can check the accuracy of their recollections.

Variation 5 Describe and compare

1   Show a class of more advanced students about 15 objects or pictures of objects and then ask them to write down what they remember, *describing the objects* in detail. It is easier and equally challenging to show the objects or pictures *one after the other* instead of at the same time.

2   When the learners have written down everything they can remember, tell them to exchange their descriptions with their neighbour.

3   Ask each learner to check their neighbour's work as you hold up the objects and pictures again. As you hold up each object, discuss with the class its character. For example:

Teacher: *What's this?*
Learner 1:   *A scarf.*
Teacher: (asking John's partner) *Did John remember it?*
Learner 1:   *Yes, he did.*
Teacher: (asking John's partner) *What did he say about it? / How did he describe it?*
Learner 1:   *He said* (reading from his partner's work) *it was red, green, yellow ... and woolly.*
Teacher: (asking the class) *Well, is it? Was he right?*
Learner 2:   *No, he wasn't. It isn't red, it's orange!*
Teacher: *Well, it's sort of red, isn't it?*
Learner 3:   *And it isn't green.*
Teacher: *Tell me when John was right and when he was wrong.*
Learner 4:   *He was right when he said that the scarf is red, yellow and woolly, and wrong when he said that it is green.*

Note

See **7.21 Kim's memory game** for Variations 6 and 7.

6.13 Would you make a good witness?

Family	REMEMBER
Language	Vocabulary of whatever pictures you show: clothes, cars, food, etc. Asking and answering questions
Preparation	Choose a picture or make a montage, big enough for the class to see, which will elicit the language you want to practise. Examples might be: *clothes* – a page from a mail-order catalogue showing five men in different clothes

> *actions* – a general photo of a scene with a lot of people doing different things
> *personal descriptions* – a montage of portraits of people

Procedure

1 Ask the learners if they think they would make good witnesses. Are they good at remembering the details of what they see? Tell them you are going to test them.

2 Show the picture to the class for twenty seconds, then turn the picture away. If the picture is not very big, walk through the class making sure that all the learners see it properly.

3 Tell the learners, working in pairs, to ask each other questions about what they remember about the picture. For example:

> *What did you see?*
> *How many people were there?*
> *What were they doing?*
> *What did they look like?*
> *How old were they?*
> *What were they wearing?*
> *What do you think they might have been saying or thinking?*
> *What colour, shape, size, etc. was the ...?*

4 Interrogate the learners to discover what they can remember about the picture.

> Teacher: *What can you remember? What was in the picture?*
> Learner 1: *There were some people.*
> Teacher: *How many people? Can you remember?*
> Learner 2: *I think there were five or six people.*
> Teacher: *What were they wearing?*
> etc.

CREATE

6.14 Change the story

Family	CREATE
Language	Writing narrative, with an emphasis on nouns
	Possibly practising other grammar points, e.g. positive and negative statements

Procedure

1 Ask learners to write a 100-word short story or description, and to underline all the nouns in their text. You may wish to channel the learners' creativity by suggesting a topic.

2 Help the class to compile a list of about twenty nouns through brainstorming.

3 Ask individual learners to read out their text, omitting the nouns. As they pause in place of a noun, the other learners supply a random noun from the list. Alternatively, each learner substitutes a noun at random into their text before reading it. The result can be very amusing, depending, of course, on comprehension of the word in context.

Note

Other language items can modified or added, for example, adjectives instead of nouns, or all positive statements can be changed to negative statements.

7 Mainly grammar

The games in this section focus on particular points of grammar and give the learners the opportunity to *experience* the language *in use* in contexts that are meaningful and enjoyable, and to practise using them over and over again. This helps the learners to understand, remember and, later, to re-use the language.

Look in the information box for each game to see what point of grammar is being focussed on. Note that many of the games are multipurpose, offering practice for a variety of language items.

For a complete list of language, in these and other games in other sections, see the Index.

DO: *MOVE, MIME, DRAW, OBEY*

7.1 Simon says

Family	DO: *OBEY*
Language	Total physical response (TPR)
	Demonstrating understanding of imperatives by ...
	Main game ... moving appropriately in response to spoken orders
	Variation 1 ... miming in response to spoken orders
	Variation 2 ... obeying spoken instructions requiring movement
	Variation 3 ... obeying written instructions requiring performance of a physical or mental task

Procedure

1 Tell the class that you are going to give them instructions. Anything Simon says that they should do, they must do exactly, but anything said without Simon's name should not be obeyed. For example:

Teacher: *Simon says, stand up!* (All the learners stand up.)
Simon says, sit down! (All the learners sit down.)
Stand up! (The learners should remain seated because the order wasn't given by Simon.)

Other useful imperatives

Open your book.	*Look sad.*
Close your book.	*Look angry.*
Wave your hand.	*Put your book on a chair.*
Jump.	*Put your chair under the table.*
Walk.	*Turn around.*
Dance.	*Touch something red.*
Say 'hello' to a neighbour.	*Touch something made of leather.*
Smile.	

2   The usual rules require a player to drop out of the game if he or she does the action when the order was not preceded by *Simon says*. However, these are the learners who need most practice in listening, so ask them to continue playing but to remember how many mistakes they made and to try to do better next time.

3   Once the game is familiar, invite learners to take over the role of Simon (i.e. your role) either with the class as a whole or in pairwork.

Note

You might like to:
— write a sentence pattern on the board to give visual support to the learners' understanding and to guide pair or group games;
— show the instructions in writing on cards instead of speaking;
— say *please* instead of *Simon says*.

Variation 1   Film director

Preparation   Choose or prepare a story outline that can be easily acted out as if for a film. It must be full of action for acting out! Alternatively, you may invite the learners to choose or create the story.

An example of a story outline
A man has a robot who shops for him, cooks for him, etc. He sends the robot to his girlfriend's house with a rose. The girlfriend falls in love with the robot, keeps it and doesn't go to see her boyfriend again.

1   When the story outline is ready, choose a learner to be the 'film director', or assume this role yourself.

2   Explain that the 'film director' will dictate the script to the rest of the learners, who must write down exactly what the 'director' says. Some sentences can summarise the situation for the 'actors' but most sentences will tell the 'actors' exactly what to do, using plenty of verbs in the imperative form. (Other language points can also be introduced, for example, adverbs, prepositions, etc.)

3   In groups, the learners mime in response to their reading of the dictated text. If every learner has prepared a story, then each learner will take it in turns over a period of days or weeks to be the 'film director' and to read out their story for the others to mime.

An example of how the beginning of the story might be written, combining descriptions and instructions

You are a man. You are lying in bed. You are ill. You are cold. Shiver! Groan! You are thirsty. You want some water. There's a glass of water on the table by the bed. You try to get the glass, but you can't. Shout, 'Robot! Come here!'

Variation 2 Magicians, hypnotists and robots

Preparation   You will need a cardboard box (optional).
               Optional: Make a magician's hat by rolling a piece of paper into a cone, or a robot costume by putting a cardboard box on somebody's head.

1   It seems natural for magicians, hypnotists or owners of robots to tell people (or robots) what to do. Invite one of the learners to take on one of these roles or do so yourself.

2   Tell the class that they must obey all orders!

Examples for a magician and for a hypnotist

Magician: *I am a magician! You are a frog! Hop! Jump! Stop! Sit down! Go to sleep! etc.*

Hypnotist: *Sit down, please. Look at my watch (swings watch). Relax. Relax. Shut your eyes. You are becoming younger and younger. You are now three years old. Stand up. Walk. Fall over a teddy bear. Cry. Shout, 'Mummy!' Say, 'Mummy! Give me some juice!' Drink the juice. Say, 'Thank you.' Sit down. Relax. Relax. You are getting older and older. Now you are yourself again.*

Variation 3 Forfeits

Preparation	Make forfeit cards or encourage the learners to help invent and write forfeits, which gives them practice in using imperatives. You will also need a cardboard box to keep the forfeit cards in.

1   Explain or demonstrate with an example what a forfeit is. (In party games someone losing or doing something wrong often has to do a forfeit. Forfeits are a form of playful punishment, and are usually expressed through imperatives.)

Examples of forfeits
Sing a song.
Stand on one leg and sing a song.
Tell a joke.
Describe an embarrassing experience.
Laugh for one minute.
Count from 100 to 1 as fast as you can.

---

2   If the class like this idea, then introduce forfeits at any time, not just in a game. Keep the cards in a *Forfeits Box*.

7.2 Can you stand on one leg?

Family	DO: *OBEY*
Language	Responding to challenges (that consist of the question *Can you …?*) by performing a physical or mental feat
Creating such challenges and issuing them to others

Procedure

1   Challenge a learner to do something. For example:
      Teacher: (challenging a learner) *Can you stand on one leg?*
      Good! Now, can you stand on one leg for one minute?
2   Try to do the challenge yourself and fail miserably, in order to amuse the class and to use the negative form:
      Teacher: *Oh, I can't stand on one leg. I can only stand on one leg for a few seconds! I can't stand on one leg for one minute!*

3   Once the learners understand the idea of the game, invite them to work
out challenges and to try them on other learners in the class.

Examples of challenges
Touch your toes.
Balance a pencil on your finger.
Pick up a pencil using your toes.
Multiply 89 by 98 in your head.
Write a sentence on the board with your eyes closed.
*Pat your head with one hand and rub your stomach round and round with the
other, both at the same time.*

7.3 Miming

Family	Do: *MIME*
Language	Miming and watching mimed actions

Speculating about mimed actions using the following tenses:

Main game Present continuous for actions in progress (e.g. *You're carrying a gun*)

Variation 1 Present continuous for actions in progress (e.g. *What am I doing?*) and present simple for routine actions (e.g. *What do I do in my job?*)

Variation 2 Present simple for actions performed at the same time every day (e.g. *What do you do at 7 o'clock?*)

Variation 3 Past simple for a sequence of completed actions recalled in sequence (e.g. *You filled a pan with water. Then you put the pan on the stove*, etc.), and connecting words (e.g. *then, next, after that*) to indicate that the actions are part of a single sequence.

Variation 4 Past continuous for a continuous, uncompleted action (e.g. *You were typing*)

Variation 5 Past continuous for a continuous action in the past (e.g. *You were reading*) interrupted by another action, expressed in the past simple (e.g. *Someone knocked on the door*)

Variation 6 Present perfect for an action implying that another action has occurred in the past (e.g. *Have you hurt your thumb?*), and past simple to identify this action (e.g. *Did you hit it?*)

Variation 7 Present perfect continuous for an action that has just been completed (e.g. *You've been sleeping*)

Variation 8 Future with *going to* for an anticipated action (e.g. *You're going to dive*)

Variation 9 Future in the past for an action anticipated in the past (e.g. *You were going to dive*)
Variation 10 Future in the past for an action anticipated in the past (e.g. *You were going to dive*) which was halted by another action (e.g. *You stopped him from diving*)
Preparation Prepare a list of actions which learners could mime.

Procedure

1 Divide the class into two teams.
2 Randomly ask one learner from one team to mime an action (or sequence of actions).
3 The mimer's team must try to guess what he or she is miming. If they guess correctly, they win a point. The mimer can nod or shake their head as the team make their guesses. For example:

Team: *You're carrying something.*
Mimer: (nods head)
Team: *Is it a gun?*
Mimer: (shakes head)
Team: *Is it a stick?*
Mimer: (nods head)

Variation 1   Present continuous and present simple

1 Invite a learner to mime a number of actions they do every day.
2 Tell them that, while miming the action, they should ask the class, *What am I doing?*
3 Once someone has guessed correctly, encourage the mimer to ask what the action might represent in terms of daily actions. For example:

Learner 1: (mimes writing) *What am I doing?*
Learner 2: *You're writing.*
Learner 1: *Yes, that's right.* (mimes reading a book) *What am I doing?*
Learner 2: *You're reading a book.*
Learner 1: *So, what do I do in my job?*
Learner 2: *You are an author, or perhaps a teacher, or a secretary.*

Variation 2   Present simple

1 Draw on the board a number of clock faces, each showing a different time of day.
2 Explain that you are going to mime what you usually do at those times on weekdays. Point at the first clock face, ask the question (before the mime,

so that the general symbolic nature of your mime is more important than the individual action) *What do I do at ... o'clock?*, then mime.

    Teacher: (pointing at the first clock) *What do I do at seven o'clock?*
                 (then miming waking up)
    Learner: *You wake up.*

3   Invite learners to take over your role once they are familiar with the game. Other verbs suitable for miming are:
get up, get dressed, get washed, brush your teeth, have breakfast, leave the house, catch a bus, get to college, start work, have a break, have lunch, leave college, get home, have a meal, go to the gym, watch TV, go to bed.

Notes

- Add variety by asking what the learners always or sometimes do at the weekends away from school.
- Ask the learners to mime what they would like to do at the different times of the day related to the clock faces, using *I would like to ... if I could.*

Variation 3 Simple past

1   Mime, or invite a learner to mime, a sequence of actions, being careful to choose actions which the learners can name.

Sequence of actions involved in preparing an egg for breakfast
Filling a pan with water, putting the pan on the stove, lighting the gas, opening the fridge door, taking out an egg, putting it in the pan, waiting for the egg to boil and looking at your watch for four minutes, taking out the egg with a spoon, cooling the egg in cold water, putting the egg into an egg cup, cracking open the egg and removing the top, putting some salt on the egg, eating the egg.

---

2   Mime all the actions and **only then** ask what you did. Make use of various connecting words, for example, *then, next, after that.*

    Teacher: (mimes the whole sequence before speaking)
                 What did I do first?
    Learner 1: *You filled a pan with water.*
    Teacher: *What did I do next?*
    Learner 2: *You put the pan on the stove.*

You can ask the learners to retell the whole series of actions.

3   Once learners are familiar with the game, encourage them to take over your role.

Note

You may wish to re-enact the sequence, but omit several actions. The learners must then say what you did and what you didn't do.

Variation 4   Past continuous

Mime a continuous, uncompleted action, and then stop and ask what you were doing.

Teacher:	(mimes typing, then stops)
	What was I doing?
Learner 1:	*You were playing the piano.*
Teacher:	*Was I playing the piano?*
Learner 2:	*No.*
Teacher:	*What was I doing?*
Learner 3:	*You were typing.*

Variation 5   Past continuous interrupted by the past simple

Invite two learners to mime. Learner 1 mimes a continuous action and then Learner 2 interrupts Learner 1.

Learner 1:	(mimes reading)
Learner 2:	(after about five seconds knocks on the door and rushes into the room and shouts, 'Fire!')
Learner 1:	*What was I doing?*
Learner 3:	*You were reading.*
Learner 2:	*Then what happened?*
Learner 4:	*You knocked on the door, opened it and shouted, 'Fire!'*

Examples of other situations for the past continuous and past simple
Reading interrupted by replying to a knock at the door.
Walking interrupted by falling over a body.
Sleeping interrupted by a dog barking.
Eating interrupted by someone knocking a glass over.
Having a bath interrupted by a telephone ringing.

Variation 6 Present perfect

Mime an action that implies that something else has happened.
Invite the class to try to guess what it is, and express this by asking a
question. For example:

Teacher:	(holds his/her thumb with an expression of pain)
Learner 1:	*Have you hurt your thumb?*
Teacher:	(nods head)
Learner 2:	*Did you hit it?*
Teacher:	(nods head)
Learner 3:	*Did you hit it with a hammer?*
Teacher:	(nods head)

Note

When the learners are unsure about what has happened, it is natural to use
the present perfect, e.g. *Have you hurt your thumb?* When it is established
that an incident has been completed, the simple past tense is more relevant,
for example, *Did you hit it?*

Examples of other situations for the present perfect
Broken something (mime: shock, dismay, regret, shaking head, looking at the
floor, picking up the pieces)
Lost something (mime: frowning, looking around and under things, exasperation)
Seen a ghost (mime: look of pop-eyed horror plus wobbling knees and possibly
pointing backwards to where the ghost was seen)
Put your fingers into something horrible (mime: constant wiping of the fingers
plus face wrinkled in disgust)

Variation 7 Present perfect continuous

Mime an action that suggests another continuous action that has just been
completed.

Teacher:	(rubbing his or her eyes and stretching) *What have I been doing?*
Learner:	*You've been sleeping.*

> **Examples of other situations for the present perfect continuous**
> Washing (mime: drying your face)
> Brushing your hair (mime: looking in the mirror and patting your hair)
> Eating (mime: wiping your lips, taking off your napkin, pushing away your plate and standing up)
> Running (mime: panting for breath, leaning forwards and putting your hands on your knees)

Variation 8 Future with *going to*

Mime an action that suggests very strongly what you are going to do next. While miming ask, *What am I going to do?*

Teacher:	(standing with your legs together and your arms outstretched together in front of you) *What am I going to do?*
Learner:	*You're going to dive.*

> **Examples of other situations to elicit the future with *going to***
> Going to brush your teeth (mime: squeeze toothpaste on to a brush and bare your teeth)
> Going to shout (mime: take a breath, put your two hands on either side of your mouth, open your mouth and move your head forwards)

Variation 9 Future in the past

Mime as for the future tense but clearly stop the mime, move to another part of the class (to place the action in the past) and then ask, *What was I going to do?*

Teacher:	(mimes 'going to dive', then stops and moves to another part of the class and even points back to where he or she was standing) *What was I going to do?*
Learner:	*You were going to dive.*

Variation 10 Future in the past and simple past

Invite all the learners, in pairs, to prepare a mime in which one learner is about to do something and then is prevented from doing so by the other learner.

Learner 1:	(mimes 'going to dive')
Learner 2:	(after about five seconds Learner 2 pulls Learner 1 backwards to stop him or her diving)
Learner 1:	*What was I going to do?*
Learner 3:	*You were going to dive.*
Learner 2:	*What did I do?*
Learner 4:	*You stopped him.*

IDENTIFY: *DISCRIMINATE, GUESS, SPECULATE*

7.4 Drama of sounds

Family	IDENTIFY
Language	**Main game** Using the present continuous in reference to actions as they are heard
	(optional) Using expressions of uncertainty (e.g. *I think someone is ..., I think it is ...*)
	(optional) Using the word *somebody* (e.g. *Somebody is/was dancing.*)
	Variation 1 Using the past continuous in reference to actions that were heard

Procedure

1   List on the board verbs the learners know which can be acted out, then identified by their sound alone.

Examples of verbs that can be identified by sound

sleeping	closing a door	coughing
dancing	drinking	eating
jumping	driving	knocking
playing football	playing a guitar	running
singing	sneezing	speaking
swimming	walking	washing
watching football		

---

2   Demonstrate the idea of the game, which is for one or two learners to make a noise to represent one of the verbs you have written on the board, while the rest of the class sit with their eyes closed and try to identify the verb. Encourage the class to call out their ideas while the action is going on, in order to contextualise the present continuous. Ask the noise-

makers to sustain the noise in order to give time for the listeners to describe their action while it is still happening.

Teacher:	*What is David doing?*
Learner 1:	*He's dancing.*
Teacher:	*Alyson! Do you think David is dancing?*
Learner 2:	*I think he's running.*

3   Once learners are familiar with the game, encourage them to play it in pairs, being sure to try to identify the verbs while the action is continuing.

Notes

*   So often the present continuous is practised in the classroom by reference to actions that are seen. In this game the learners close their eyes, listen and try to interpret what they hear.
*   You may like to practise the use of *someone*, for example, *Someone is coughing. I think it is John.*

Variation 1   Mystery action and person
Follow the same game procedure as above, asking the question *after the action has stopped* in order to contextualise the past continuous.

Teacher:	*What did you hear?*
Learner 1:	*Someone was coughing.*
Teacher:	*Who was it?*
Learner 1:	*I think it was John.*

Note

You may like to increase the game element by awarding one point for any learner who volunteers an idea and two points for the learner who guesses correctly.

7.5   Telepathy (pictures)

Family	IDENTIFY
Language	Asking questions about the content of hidden pictures using the present continuous (e.g. *Is he running?*), present perfect (*Has she just dropped a plate?*) or future tense (e.g. *Is he going to jump?*), or emphasising another language point (e.g. adjectives: *Is it a green apple?*)
Preparation	Prepare or procure six to eight picture cards of, for example, actions. (It is better to have all the pictures showing either a male or a female.)

Procedure

1 Make sure the learners know the picture cards in your hand. They should be able to remember all of them.

2 Discuss telepathy with the class in the mother tongue for a few moments, raising interest in whether or not there is any truth in it.

3 Say that you will do an experiment. Select one of the picture cards at random and show it to only half the class. Tell them they must concentrate on the card, and try to send out telepathic signals about what the person in the picture is doing.

4 Tell the other half of the class that you will give them three chances to receive the telepathic signals. It is then inevitable for people to feel the need to try it again. Do it perhaps five times, with three chances each time. Each time record if the 'message' was received within the three attempts. For example:

> Learner 1: *Is he swimming?*
> Teacher: *No.*
> Learner 2: *Is he running?*
> Teacher: *Yes! Well done.*

5 Then suggest that the same experiment be done in pairs. Each learner should draw three or four stick people showing different actions. (Or they might write down three or four short sentences evoking actions in the present perfect.) Then one learner in each pair takes both sets of drawings and, hiding them from the other learner behind a book, places his/her finger on one of them. The other learner then has three guesses.

Notes

- You could ask the learners to do the experiment ten times with the utmost concentration. They should count how many times the right guess is made within the first three attempts.
- This same game can be used for practising areas of vocabulary and, of course, then involves reading the texts and thinking about them. See **5.2 Telepathy (texts)**.

7.6 Random sounds

Family	IDENTIFY: *SPECULATE*
Language	Speculating orally and/or in writing about the sources of sounds, using the past continuous, simple past, expressions of uncertainty (e.g. *I thought I heard a ...*) and/or expressions of speculation (e.g. *I think I could hear ...*).

Procedure

1 Ask the learners to close their eyes, perhaps even to rest their head on their arms. Invite them to listen carefully to every sound they can hear, and to try to identify the sounds. They should be listening for all the 'natural' noises of the classroom, the building, and outside.

2 Let everyone listen for two or three minutes, and then write down what they heard.

3 Then ask them about what they heard. For example:

> Learner 1: *I heard some girls.*
> Teacher: *What were they doing?*
> Learner 1: *They were talking and laughing.*
> Teacher: *What did you hear, Mario?*
> Learner 2: *I think I heard a plane.*

4 Alternatively, you can ask the learners to describe the noises *as they hear them* in order to contextualise the present continuous. For example:

> Learner 1: *I can hear some girls.*
> *I can hear some girls playing.*
> *They are laughing and calling to each other. I think they are playing with a ball. Yes, I can hear it (bouncing).*
> Learner 2: *I think I can hear a plane. It's probably coming into the airport.*

Note

Being able to use the present continuous depends on the particular sound continuing long enough to be able to comment on it.

7.7 Dramatised sequence of sounds

Family	IDENTIFY
Language	Acting out a series of actions with a co-actor, following instructions given in the imperative
	Listening to a series of events without watching them, then narrating them, using one or more of the following tenses: past simple, past continuous, present simple, present continuous, present perfect, future (with *going to*)
	Writing scripts for a series of actions featuring two actors, using the imperative
Preparation	Write down a sequence of actions on a piece of paper.
	When getting ready to play the game for the first time with a class, prepare two learners to demonstrate.

1 Ask everyone to close their eyes and put their head on their arms.
2 Select two learners, and give them each a copy of the sequence of actions you have written so they know what to do. (See below for an example.) If your class has never done such a thing before, it would be better to prepare your two actors before the lesson begins.

Example of a sequence of actions
A – *Sing for 20 seconds.*
B – *Listen to A for 20 seconds and then shout, 'Shut up!'*
A – *Begin to cry. Cry for about 20 seconds.*
B – *Say, 'I'm sorry.' Then walk across the room and out of the door. Shut the door.*

---

3 Let the two learners act out the sound script you have given them. Before the class open their eyes, ask A and B to return to their places.

      Teacher: *What happened?*
      Learner 1: *Brian was singing.*
      Learner 2: *Then Susan shouted, 'Shut up!'*
      Learner 3: *Then Brian cried.*
      Teacher: *Then what happened?*
      Learner 4: *Susan said, 'I'm sorry.'*
      Teacher: *What happened then?*
      Learner 5: *Susan walked out of the room.*

4   If there is some confusion over the sequence of events, tell the class to close their eyes again and ask the two learners to repeat their performance.

5   Once the sequence is correctly reported, ask everyone to watch as the performers present it one last time. Comment on it as it happens using the present continuous and then ask for a description of the whole sequence using past tenses.

6   Ask the learners, in pairs or groups, to prepare, write and present their own sequences. Show them how to write the instructions, using imperatives, as in the example given above.

Note

Any of the sound drama sequences may be recorded. The advantage of recording the dramas is that background sound effects can be added, even if it is in an amateurish way, and this invites more creativity and participation by the learners. Also the recording can be replayed very easily. Sound recordings of mini sound dramas can be used to promote the use of all the tenses.

Using sound recordings of a mini drama to focus on different tenses

Present continuous
Ensure that each action continues long enough on the recording to be identified using the present continuous while the sound of the action is continuing.

Present simple
Present a sequence of actions which are established, e.g. daily actions or actions related to a particular activity. The question you ask then prompts the use of the present simple.

Teacher: *Here is Julia's Sunday. What does she do every Sunday morning?*
(sound of gentle snoring)
Learner 1:   *She sleeps.*
Teacher: *Yes, she sleeps. She sleeps until what time?*
(sound of clock chiming eleven)
Learner 2:   *Until eleven o'clock.*
etc.

Future with *going to*

Once the learners are familiar with the recording, you can keep stopping the recording and asking them what is going to happen next.

Simple past

You can pause the recording periodically to ask learners to report on short actions that have just occurred, or wait until the end of the recording to ask about them.

Past continuous

After listening to the recording, you can ask the learners to tell you about longer or repetitive actions.

Present perfect

You can pause the recording as an event is completed, and ask *What has just happened?*

7.8 Paper fortune-teller

Family	IDENTIFY
Language	Asking questions with *Who* ...? and *What* ...? Reading and writing sentences containing reference to the future with *will*
Preparation	Make a paper fortune-teller. This device, folded in paper, is known to children in many countries. If you are not sure how it is made, ask some children aged nine or ten! Write names and numbers on the outside surfaces, or try using colours instead. (The fortune-teller should then be opened and closed according to the number of letters in the colour, for example g-r-e-e-n, five times.) On the inside write eight sentences referring to the future.

Procedure

1 Show the class your fortune-teller and tell one or two fortunes. The usual exchange between English children is as follows:

A: *Who do you love?* (referring to one of the names on the fortune-teller)

B: *Simon.*

A: *S-I-M-O-N* (alternately opens and shuts the device as he or she says each letter). *What number do you want?*

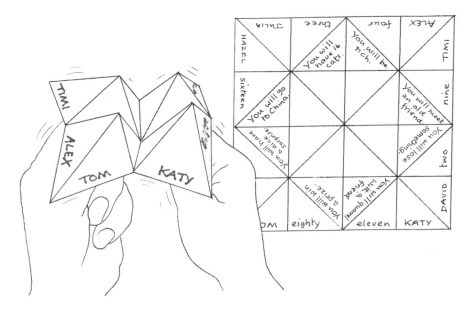

B: 8.

A: 1, 2, 3, 4, 5, 6, 7, 8 (alternately opens and shuts the device as he or she says each number)
What number do you want now?

B: 3.

A: (opens the flap with the number 3 written on it and reads out the fortune written beneath) *You will have 16 cats!*

2 On the assumption that at least some people in the class will know how to make the device and will help those who don't, ask everyone to prepare eight appropriate original sentences referring to the future. For example:

You will go to China.

You will win a prize.

3 Organise the making of the devices so that each learner has one, writes eight sentences referring to the future (using *will*) in the middle, and writes names and numbers on the flaps.

Note

The future tense using *will* suggests a dispassionate, cool prediction or even a command. The *going to* future tense brings the future action vividly into the present.

Variation 1 Inventing fortunes for friends

1 Ask learners to form groups of four or five, then to write a fortune or prediction for each member of their group. In other words, each learner writes three or four fortunes.
2 When the learners have completed this first step, invite them to give each of the fortunes to the learner concerned.
3 Invite learners to read their fortunes out to their group and comment, for example, on whether some of them are the same, or just what they had hoped for, or highly unlikely.

Notes

- The learners need not know each other well. People love having their fortunes told, even if the prediction is clearly without any foundation!
- At some future time you can ask if the fortune telling proved to be correct or not. This invites a natural use of the future in the past tense and the simple past tense.

Teacher:	*John said you were going to meet a strange person. Did you meet a strange person?*
Learner:	*Yes, I did.*
Teacher:	*What happened?*

7.9 Why did they say that?

Family Language	IDENTIFY
	Imagining and writing explanations for exclamations and questions Listening to descriptions of extraordinary circumstances, and reacting orally with an appropriate exclamation or question

Procedure

1 Write ten exclamations and/or questions on the board.

Examples of exclamations and questions

No!	*Good luck!*	*Really!*
Yes!	*Good luck?*	*Really?*
Sorry!	*Bad luck!*	*Wow!*
Sorry?	*Bad luck?*	*Not now!*
Never mind!	*Careful!*	*Of course!*
Never mind?	*Careful?*	

---

2 Invite pairs to write a sentence explaining a reason for somebody saying one of these exclamations or questions. Ask learners to take turns reading out their sentences, and the rest of the class to identify which exclamation or question is being referred to in each case.

Example 1
Explanation: *A pet owner said to a friend, 'Would you like to kiss my tarantula?'*
Exclamation: *No!*

Example 2
Explanation: *A man told his friend he was going to get married. His friend said, 'Good luck!' And the man said …*
Question: *Good luck?*

---

3 Ask the learners to take another exclamation and to invent an even funnier reason.
4 Once they are ready, invite the learners to stand up and mill about, reading out their extraordinary explanations and asking the other learners to identify the exclamation it refers to.

7.10 Objects in a box

Family	IDENTIFY
Language	Naming objects and describing them in as many ways and as much detail as possible (using adjectives, making true statements about them)
	Using possessives to indicate the owners of objects
	(optional) Guessing the name of a hidden object, using the question *Have you got a …?*
Preparation	You will need a box or bag big enough to hold 10 small objects.

Procedure

1 Go round the classroom picking up about ten small objects. Ask the learners to name each object before you put it into the box or bag.

2 Put your hand into the box, take hold of one of the objects but do not take it out.

Teacher:	*What have I got in my hand?*
Learner 1:	*A comb.* (guessing, because the learners cannot see what the teacher is holding)
or:	*The comb.* (if only one comb was put in the box)
Teacher:	*No.*
Learner 2:	*A/The watch.*
Teacher:	*Yes.*

You may ask learners to guess what you're holding by telling them to ask you *Have you got a ...?*

3 Explain that the learner who guessed correctly has won the object, unless someone else can call out something true about it before you hand it over. Start to walk towards the learner to give them the object, and immediately change direction if another learner says something true about it, for example:

Learner 1:	*It's black!* (walk towards Learner 1)
Learner 2:	*It's small!* (walk towards Learner 2)

4 Learners may continually attempt to 'win' the object by calling out true statements:

Learner 3:	*It's a silver watch.* (walk towards Learner 3)
Learner 4:	*It's fast.* (walk towards Learner 4)
Learner 5:	*It's ticking.* (walk towards Learner 5)
Learner 6:	*It's not Big Ben.* (walk towards Learner 6)
Learner 7:	*It's like a person. It has a face and two hands.* (walk towards Learner 7 and give it to Learner 7 if no other learner calls out anything before you get there)

5 When the game is over, make use of possessive forms in returning the objects to their owners.

Teacher:	*Whose is this?*
Learner:	*It's mine/his/John's.*

7.11 Where's the mouse?

Family	IDENTIFY
Language	**Main game** Asking questions using *Are you* + preposition + place (e.g. *Are you on top of the cupboard?*) in an attempt to locate someone
	Variation Making suggestions using *Let's* + verb + object + preposition + place (e.g. *Let's hide the watch on top of the cupboard.*) Asking questions using *Is it* + preposition + place (e.g. *Is it under the table?*) in an attempt to locate something
	(optional) Asking questions using the present perfect (e.g. *Have you hidden it near the door?*) or the passive form (e.g. *Is it hidden at the back of the classroom?* or *Has it been hidden at the back of the classroom?*)
Preparation	(optional) You may like to bring a picture showing lots of places in which a mouse could hide (see step 1).

Procedure

1 Invite the learners to take it in turns to imagine being a mouse. The 'mouse' should think of a hiding place in the room, or in a larger place, for example *the school* or *the town*. (Alternatively, show the class a picture and ask the 'mouse' to imagine where in the picture he or she is hiding.) Ask the 'mouse' to write down their location on a bit of paper. (This will prevent the 'mouse' from cheating!)

2 Challenge the other learners to ask questions to try to find where 'the mouse' is, for example:

> Learner 2: *Are you in the cupboard?*
> 'Mouse': No.
> Learner 3: *Are you under the desk?*
> 'Mouse': No.

Variation 1 Hiding place

1 Send one or two learners out of the room. Discuss with the class what small object they would like to hide and where it should be hidden. For example:

> Learner 1: *Let's hide this watch.*
> Learner 2: *Let's hide this coin.*
> Learner 3: *Let's hide it under the box of chalk.*
> Learner 4: *Let's hide it in the cupboard.*

2   When the object is hidden, call the learner(s) in and challenge them to find the object by asking questions. For example:

Learner 1:   *Is it at the front of the room?*
Class: *Yes.*
Learner 1:   *Is it on top of the cupboard?*
Class: *No.*

At an intermediate level, the learner(s) who went outside the classroom can be asked to use the present perfect (e.g. *Have you hidden it near the door?*) or the passive form (e.g. *Is it hidden at the back of the classroom?* or *Has it been hidden at the back of the classroom?*).

3   When the 'seekers' guess correctly, they should go to the place, find the object, hold it up and say: *Is it this (watch)?*

Note

As so often in games, you may decide that it will help the learners if you give examples of phrases on the board for them to make use of.

7.12 Twenty questions

Family	IDENTIFY
Language	Asking questions to acquire information in an attempt to reveal the identity of an unknown animal, person, place, object or idea

Procedure

1   Think of an animal, a person, a place, an object or an idea, and introduce the game as follows:

Teacher: *I am thinking of something. It is an animal / a person / a place / an object / an event / an idea.* (Choose the most appropriate label.)

Alternatively, once the learners are familiar with *Twenty questions,* you can invite one of them to start off the game. This is an advantage, because it gives you the opportunity of showing the class how to narrow down the range of possibilities.

2   Invite the players to put twenty questions to the acting 'question master' in an attempt to discover what they are thinking of. The questions must be put so that they can be answered by *Yes* or *No.*

Examples of questions that narrow down the possibilities

Is it bigger/smaller than a car?
Can you eat it?
Have you got one?
Would you normally find one in a house?
Is it made of (wood)?
Can it be easily broken?

---

3 Award a point to the learners if they discover what it is in less than twenty questions. Otherwise, the point goes to the 'question master'.

7.13 Flashing a picture

Family IDENTIFY

Language Describing pictures of which one has only seen brief glimpses, using certain tenses (as determined by your choice of picture and influenced by the questions you use to guide the learners), for example:
Past continuous: *A man. What was he doing? He was running.*
Present continuous: *A man. What is he doing? He is sitting in a chair.*
Going to future: *A man. What is he going to do? He is going to jump off a building.*
Variation Predicting the contents of a text based on brief glimpses of its contents, indications as to its general meaning, as well as familiarity with word order and the habitual grouping of certain words. You can choose a text to focus on a grammatical point or a function.

Preparation You will need a picture (from a magazine or drawn on paper or OHP transparency) no bigger than magazine-page size. Choose or draw a picture that consists of reasonably simple shapes rather than intricate details, and that requires the language you want the learners to practise in order to describe it. Mount paper pictures on card in order to be able to flick them over quickly.

Procedure

1 Explain that you are going to test the learners' ability to see at great speed.
2 Hold the picture towards you and upside down, and spin it very quickly indeed so that the learners receive only a momentary flash of it. (Practise this at home! The first few 'flashes' should be really fast!) Make sure that

everyone can see it – there should be no heads in the way and the angle should not be too acute for learners on each side of the class.

3 Ask the class what they saw. Some will have seen nothing, but others will have seen some colours and someone might, amazingly, have seen the gist of the whole picture.

4 Continue to give the occasional flash, perhaps a little slower, and gradually work towards a correct description in broad terms. At no point should you confirm or deny the learners' observations. Just provoke the differences between their contributions in order to promote opinion gaps and a reason for listening and speaking.

> Learner 1: *There is/was a woman.*
> Teacher: *What is/was she wearing?*
> Learner 1: *I don't know, but it is/was yellow.*
> Teacher: *Yellow?*
> Learner 2: *Orange.*

5 Finally, show the picture.

Variation 1 Flashing a text

Preparation Find or write a short text which contains an example of the grammatical point you wish to focus on. Write the text on a card or OHP transparency.

Flash the text and invite students to reconstruct it, based on the words they have glimpsed.

7.14 How long is it?

Family	IDENTIFY: *SPECULATE, COMPARE*
Language	Using comparatives (*bigger, smaller*), superlatives (*widest, narrowest*) and expressing conjecture (e.g. *I think…*) in speculating about, then judging …
	Main game … the relative lengths of lines
	Variation 1 … the relative widths of angles
	Variation 2 … the relative area of squares
	The main game also involves the use of possessives (e.g. *John's line*).

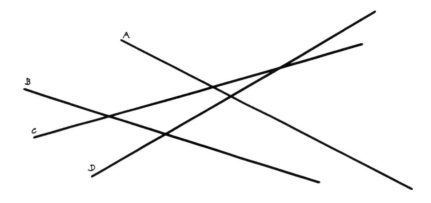

Procedure

1   Invite four or five learners to take it in turns to draw a line on the board. Each line should be in a different colour, of a different length and be straight. (The lengths should not be too varied.) It helps the game if the lines are crossed.

2   Challenge the class to judge which is the longest, and which the shortest line. For example:

　　　Teacher:　　*Which is the longest line, Rachel?*
　　　Learner 1:　*John's line.*
　　　Teacher:　　*What do you think, Robin?*
　　　Learner 2:　*I think Mary's line is the longest.*

You will find it natural to use comparatives as you discuss the opinions put forward. For example:

　　　Teacher:　　*Don't you think the red line is longer than the green line, Robin?*

Encourage the learners to use the comparative form by questioning them in the following way:

> Teacher: *I think the blue line is longer than the brown line. What do you think, David?*
>
> Learner 1: *I think it's shorter.*

3 After some further discussion, ask each learner to write down their judgements, for example:

> *The green line is the shortest line.*
> *The red line is longer than the green line.*
> *The brown line is longer than the red line.*
> *The yellow line is the longest.*

4 Finally, measure the lines and write the measurements next to them.

5 Staying with the same game and language practice, guide the learners into individual work, and then into pair work as follows.

Ask each learner to use a ruler to draw a number of coloured lines on a piece of paper. Below the lines they should write a number of sentences, some true and some deliberately false, concerning the relative lengths, for example:

> *The red line (A) is longer than the green line (C).*
> *The brown line (B) is longer than the black line (D).*
> *The green line is shorter than the brown line.*

6 Tell the learners to exchange their papers with a partner, who must determine, judging by eye, which of the statements are true and which false.

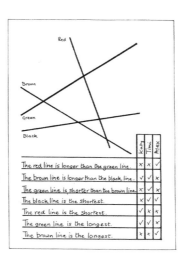

Here is an example of a student's page.

Variation 1 How wide is it?

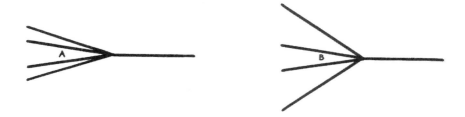

Angle A is wider than angle B. True or false?

Preparation	Draw the above diagram on the board or prepare it on a poster before the lesson.

1 Ask the class as a whole whether angle A is wider or narrower than angle B.
2 Measure it, cover the outer lines and explain the illusion.
3 Encourage each learner to draw several examples of this type of diagram, adjusting them slightly so that they are not necessarily the same size, and then to make a true or a false statement that their partner must judge.

Variation 2 How big is it?

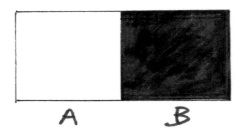

A   B

True or not true?
Rectangle B is bigger than rectangle A.

Preparation	Draw the above diagram on the board or prepare it on a poster before the lesson.

1   Ask the class as a whole whether rectangle A is bigger or smaller in area than rectangle B. In order to decide exactly how big each rectangle is, measure two adjacent sides and multiply them to establish the area.
2   Encourage each learner to draw several examples of this type of diagram, adjusting them slightly so that they are not necessarily the same size, and then to make a true or a false statement that their partner must judge.

DESCRIBE

7.15 Riddles

Family	DESCRIBE
Language	**Main game** Writing riddles using present simple questions and statements, and solving riddles presented orally **Variation 1** Writing riddles using present simple questions and statements, and solving riddles presented in writing **Variation 2** Asking questions in the present simple about the characteristics of an unknown object, in an attempt to identify it

Procedure

1   Launch this activity by demonstrating the idea of a riddle for the class: describe something and then ask the class to say what it is. Make the first example very easy! For example:

> Teacher: *It is made of glass. It is a rectangle. You can see through it. What is it?*
>
> Class: *A window!*
>
> Teacher: *Yes!*
>
> Teacher: *It is an animal. It has got four legs and a tail. It barks. It eats meat and bones.*

2   If you would like, brainstorm on to the board words and phrases that are useful for describing things (or people) that are found in particular places, for example, the classroom, a busy street, a farmer's field. Ask the learners to write five riddles using a selection of these words and phrases.
3   Invite learners to take it in turns to describe something for the other learners to identify.

Useful language for describing people and animals
It is / has ...
It lives in / for ...
It eats / drinks ...
It likes / doesn't like ...
It can ...

Note

You can make this game more challenging by limiting to three, for example, the number of sentences allowed in the description.

Variation 1 Riddle and write

1   Invite each pair or small group of learners to write a five-line riddle describing an object, place, person or animal. Ask them to write their riddles on A5 paper and display them on the wall or on a table. Here is an example of a riddle for *cat*.
> *I am smaller than a big dog.*
> *I am faster than a fat dog.*
> *I can climb like a squirrel.*
> *I like to lie in the sun.*
> *I drink milk and I purr.*

2   Invite all the learners to tour the classroom, reading and trying to solve all the other riddles.

3   Finally, make a book of riddles.

Variation 2 Riddles and questions

Preparation	Think of several words (object, place, person or animal) that can be the basis of a riddle and write each on a separate card. If the learners need a lot of support, write about 10 questions on a poster to help guide their queries.

1   Give a word card to one of the more proficient learners in the class, who must pretend to be the person or thing on the card. Tell the class:

Teacher: *Tom is pretending to be someone or something! I wonder what he is. Is he a table? Is he a chair? Is he a tree or a bird? Let's ask him questions and find out. Here are some questions you can ask.* (Put up your poster of questions.)

?????????? **What am I?** ??????????

I am smaller than a big dog.
Am I a mouse?

I am faster than a fat dog.
Am I a rabbit?

I can hear very well. Am I a bat?

I can see in the night. Am I a fox?

What am I?

??????????????????

2   Encourage the learners to ask the 'pretender' questions, until they can name the word.

Learner 1:   *How big are you?*
'Pretender':   *I am small.*

An opening question if you don't identify the category yourself
Are you an object, place, person or animal?

Examples of questions about an object
How big are you?
What are you made of?
Are you valuable?

Examples of questions about an animal
Where do you live?
What do you eat?
How big are you?
Can you climb trees?
Do people like you?

Examples of questions about a person
Are you alive?
Are you a man or a woman?
What do you do?
What do you look like?
Do you appear on television?

Examples of questions about a place
Are you a building?
Where are you?
What do people do there?

CONNECT: *COMPARE, MATCH, GROUP*

7.16 Pelmanism (grammar)

Family	CONNECT: *MATCH*
Language	Matching cards containing text and/or pictures, using the language point emphasised by the set of cards utilised. (*Any* language point can be focussed on in this game!)

Main game Matching pairs of cards visually, challenged by the hiding of the cards' faces and the need to memorise the location of those glimpsed.

Variation 1 Matching pairs of cards visually, challenged by the hiding of the cards' faces and the need to memorise the location of those glimpsed. Demonstrating understanding of the meaning of pairs of cards by making a sentence containing the words in question.

Variation 2 Searching for the owner of a card matching one's own by offering and requesting information orally and visually.

Variation 3 Preparing question and answer cards, and challenging others to match them orally or visually.

Preparation Make a set of 10 pairs of cards for each group of three to four players. Alternatively, ask the learners to make the cards themselves. The latter is both time-saving for you and more involving for the learners. The pairs of cards can relate to each other in a range of ways, according to the language needs of the learners. (See below for examples of different types of matching pairs.)

Examples of matching pairs

English word / gapped sentence (e.g. *on* / *We play football … Sundays.*)

adjective / comparative form (e.g. *happy* / *happier*)

noun / adjectival form (e.g. *help* / *helpful*)

adjectives / adverbial form (e.g. *slow* / *slowly*)

infinitive / past tense form (e.g. *stand* / *stood*)

word / opposite (e.g. *kind* / *unkind*)

two halves of one sentence pattern (e.g. *I get up* / *every day at seven o'clock.*)

active / passive (e.g. *hear* / *be heard*)

sentence / reported speech version (e.g. *What's wrong?* / *He asked me what was wrong.*)

two halves of a phrasal verb (e.g. *look* / *after*)

part of speech / example (e.g. *past tense* / *ran*)

invention / date (e.g. *telephone* / *was invented in 1876*)

Note

This game is called Pelmanism in Britain and Concentration in North America.

Procedure

1 Invite the learners to form groups of three or four. Give each group a set of cards, and help them become familiar with the pairs. A simple way to do this is to invite them to muddle all the cards face up and then see how quickly they can pair them together.

2 Ask the learners to shuffle the cards and lay them *face down* so that the pictures and/or writing on the cards cannot be seen. It doesn't matter if the players see the cards being put down and if they try to remember where the pairs were placed.

3 The first player then picks up two of the cards. If they think their cards match, they make some appropriate comment to the others, before picking them up. For example:

Player 1: (pointing to the back of a card) *Apple!* (turns over the picture
... if it is the picture of the apple then they leave it turned over)
(pointing to the back of another card) *The apple has been
eaten!* (turns over the card ... if the picture and the text make a
pair, the player leaves them turned over)

4 If the others agree that the cards are a pair, the player keeps them and
takes another turn.

5 When two cards are picked up which do not match, they must be shown
to the other players and replaced in exactly the same position from which
they were taken. Then the next player has a turn.

6 This continues until all the cards have been paired off. The player with
the most pairs is the winner.

Notes

- This is one of the richest families of language-learning activities ... and so
easy to offer to the learners. Note that it is possible to do matching
entirely by reading and writing. It is not a minor point that we are
suggesting that each item is written on its own card. The physical
handling of these cards is a key and a gateway to better learning for many
people. They can 'get a grasp' of the idea.

- Matching cards, once prepared, can be used again and again. If you
laminate them they will last even longer and look smart.

- Card-matching games can be used by you in classwork, but they are so
flexible that you can also have packets of them ready to give to
individuals or groups of learners who finish activities before the others.

- To reduce arguments, make a key for each set of cards so that the learners
can check against the key if there is any dispute.

- You can complicate the game by making the examples very close or by
including extra word cards that have no partner.

- In most countries small printing houses throw away thousands of strips
of card. These are perfect for matching card games.

Variation 1 Phrasal verbs

In this variation, the cards used should be verbs that can be paired with
prepositions to make phrasal verbs.

1 Allow play to proceed as in the main game above.

2 Challenge learners who succeed in turning over two cards that match to
make a sentence with the phrasal verb. If the sentence is grammatically

correct they win a point. You might like to ask the learners to write down their sentences in order to allow you to judge their correctness.

Variation 2 Knowledge quiz

1 Invite pairs of learners to create sets of cards containing general knowledge questions and answers.
2 Ask the learners to exchange sets of cards with each other and attempt to answer the questions, either orally or by physically matching the cards.
3 If a set of questions is particularly difficult for the pairs who try to answer them, then the same set of questions can be given to the class as a whole.

Here are three types of subject with a few examples:

General knowledge

Where is the Taj Mahal?	*It's in India.*
Where was Tolstoy born?	*In Russia (at Yasnaya Polyana).*
What is the capital of Scotland?	*Edinburgh.*
How many players are there in a cricket team?	*Eleven.*
Who painted 'Guernica'?	*Picasso.*

Jokes

Which king of England wore the largest shoes?	*The one with the largest feet.*
What can you have when someone has taken it?	*A photograph.*
What is the difference between a nail and a bad boxer?	*One is knocked in, the other is knocked out.*
Waiter, there is a dead fly in my soup!	*Yes, sir, it's the hot water which has killed it.*

Cause and effect

What would happen if the sun lost its heat?	*All living things would die.*
What happens if we combine oxygen and hydrogen?	*We get water.*
What happens when we add blue to yellow?	*It turns green.*

7.17 Bingo grammar

Family
Language

CONNECT: *MATCH*

Matching randomly-chosen information offered orally with written or pictorial information on cards that can be manipulated by hand Focussing on *any* language point.

Main game Making sentences in the present continuous indicating physical actions (e.g. *A woman is smiling*), and doing sketches that represent these sentences

Matching spoken sentences with sketches

Variation 1 Matching spoken determiners (*a, an, some, any*) with written names of foods.

Variation 2 Matching spoken words with written names of parts of speech (e.g. *verb, article, noun, adverb, adjective, pronoun, preposition, conjunction*, etc.; *verb of motion, verb – past tense, plural noun, singular noun*, etc.).

Procedure

1 Brainstorm twenty sentences in the present continuous indicating physical actions and write them on the board, for example:

A footballer is kicking the ball.
A woman is smiling.
A boy is shouting.

2 Ask the learners to make a Bingo grid by dividing a piece of paper into four squares. Tell them to choose any four of the sentences and illustrate them with quick sketches, one in each square. Give them exactly 10 seconds to make each of the drawings. You must do this or the learners will not be ready at the same time.

3 The game is then played as follows: you call out the sentences in random order and the learners cross out the pictures sketched on their Bingo grid if they illustrate the sentences you call out.

4 When a learner has crossed out all of his or her pictures, he or she shouts *Bingo!*

5 Play the game several times to give each learner the chance to do well and, of course, to give more practice in the chosen language form.

Note

By using pictures, the learners' attention is focussed on the meaning of the sentences.

Variation 1 Bingo parts of speech

Preparation	Make a list of words or set of cards representing different parts of speech.

Procedure

1 Ask the learners to draw a Bingo grid of four or six squares (or 'boxes') on an A4 piece of paper.

2 Tell each learner to decide which parts of speech they are going to listen out for and write one into the top of each of their boxes. They might choose from: verb, article, noun, adverb, adjective, pronoun, preposition, conjunction, etc. Such distinctions as 'verb of motion', 'verb – past tense', 'plural noun', 'singular noun', etc. may of course be added with your guidance. You can in this way give practice in the recognition and identification of *any* parts of speech. A learner might decide to have more than one box for a given part of speech.

3   As you call out words, the learners write them into the correct square on
    their grid. They only need one word in each box in order to say *Bingo!*
4   Make sure you keep a record of the words you have read out.

For more matching games and topics that can be used in the Bingo game see
the examples of matching pairs in **7.16 Pelmanism (grammar)**. In *Bingo*, you
call out one of the pairs, and the learners tick off the other one if it is on their
Bingo grid.

ORDER

7.18 Delete a word

Family	ORDER
Language	Deleting words from a sentence without compromising grammatical correctness
	Reading out loud, using appropriate stress, rhythm and intonation
	Discussion of meanings and changes in meanings
	Making suggestions; agreeing and disagreeing
Preparation	Select or write a complex sentence appropriate to the proficiency level of your learners.
	(optional) Copy the sentence on to strips of card, one card per word. (Although preparing strips of card requires a little preparation time, it is preferable to using the board since the game can be played more easily this way.)

Procedure

1   Write a complex sentence on the board, or on strips of card (one word per
    strip), which you should then affix to a wall or display board.
2   Tell the learners that the object of the game is to take the given sentence
    and reduce it, step by step, to the shortest possible length that is still
    grammatically correct and makes sense.
3   At each step, a deletion must be made that entails (a) the removal of one
    word, or (b) the removal of two or three consecutive words. (Two or
    three words that are separated in the sentence by other words may *not* be
    deleted.) The punctuation of the sentence may be altered at any time as
    required, and the meaning of the increasingly short sentences that result
    from the deletions may also be altered, i.e. may be different from the
    meaning of preceding sentences. (It would, in fact, be virtually impossible
    to play this game without altering meanings!) Deletions that would make
    the sentence ungrammatical are, of course, not allowed.

4   Encourage the learners, working together as a class, to suggest which word or words to delete. When they do this they should also read out the new sentence or phrase that would result from the deletion, using appropriate stress, rhythm and intonation, so that the others can *hear* as well as see before judging whether the suggestions are acceptable.

If strips of card are used, as recommended above, it is easier to manage discussion of suggestions from the class as to which word or words might be deleted. Suggestions which prove unacceptable can be more quickly corrected – by you replacing the word strips which you have just removed – than if you used board and chalk, which might entail a good deal of rubbing out and writing in of words.

5   Towards the end, it may be a matter of debate as to whether what is left constitutes a valid sentence or phrase. Once everyone agrees that no further deletions can be made, announce that they have brilliantly succeeded in reducing the sentence!

Example of a text for reduction
Consider the following sentence, from a children's version of *Robinson Crusoe*:
Nearly everything in the ship was spoiled by the sea water, though I managed to save some casks of wine, a kettle, a spade, an axe and a pair of tongs.

Example of how the text might be reduced
One word removed:
Everything in the ship was spoiled by the sea water, though I managed to save some casks of wine, a kettle, a spade, an axe and a pair of tongs.

A later step:
The ship was spoiled by water. I managed to save wine and tongs.
After yet more deletions, the sentences can be further reduced to:
The ship managed.

7.19 Word by word

Family	ORDER
Language	Making phrases and sentences orally, word by word, in cooperation with others, paying particular attention to grammar rules

Procedure

1 Tell the learners to form groups, then ask the first player in each group to say a word. Alternatively, say a word yourself, so that all groups start off the same.

2 Choose one learner in each group to act as secretary and write down the first word, then the rest of the words as play advances.

3 Ask the next learner to add a word that will make some sort of sense when put either in front of the first word or after it, and to say the two words together for the other players in the group to hear.

4 The following player has to add a word that will make sense when put *in front of* or *after* the previous two words, and to say the resulting phrase of three words.

5 Encourage the learners to continue building the sentence orally, word by word, passing it round and round the group in this manner until they have made as long a sentence as possible. For example:

    Learner 1: *Cat.*
    Learner 2: *Black cat.*
    Learner 3: *Black cat climbs.*
    Learner 4: *The black cat climbs.*
    Learner 5: *The black cat climbs high ...*

6 Finally, in a class discussion, ask all the group secretaries to read out their completed sentences, and the rest of the class should judge as to whether they are grammatically well formed (even if incomplete) and make sense.

REMEMBER

7.20 Picture the scene

Family	REMEMBER
Language	**Main game** Describing a picture from memory, focussing on people's appearance, actions and surroundings, using the past simple (e.g. *I saw a man*) and past continuous (e.g. *He was standing at a bus stop*)

Variation 1 Preparing and asking questions about the appearance, actions and surroundings of people in a picture, and answering this type of question, using the past simple (e.g. *What did you see in the picture? I saw a man*) and past continuous (e.g. *What was he doing? He was standing at a bus stop*)

Variation 2 Describing from memory what someone was wearing using the past simple (e.g. *She had a green sweater on*) and past continuous (e.g. *He was wearing a baseball cap*)

Variation 3 Describing the appearance and actions of performers from memory, using the past simple (e.g. *They stole the box of chalk*) and past continuous (e.g. *They were wearing ski goggles*)

Preparation Find a picture of a busy street scene, for example, from a magazine, tourist brochure, road safety publication, etc.

Procedure

1 Before showing the picture, ask if any of the learners have witnessed an accident or crime in the street. Discuss with the class the difficulties of being a reliable witness.

2 Then tell them that you are going to show them a picture of a street for a few seconds and that they must try to remember as much of it as they can.

3 If the picture is big, show it from the front of the class. If it is small, walk slowly about the class, letting the learners look at it as you pass.

4 Hide the picture and ask the learners to tell you what they saw. You may have to prompt the learners or cross-check their answers. For example:

Teacher: *What did you see in the picture? What can you remember?*

Learner 1: *I saw a man …*

Teacher: *Yes. What was he doing?*

Learner 1: *He was standing at a bus stop.*

Teacher: *Was anyone else standing at the bus stop?*

Learner 2: *Yes, a boy.*

Teacher: *Can you tell me what the boy was wearing?*

Learner 2: *He was wearing a T-shirt and jeans.*

Teacher: *Was he really wearing a T-shirt?*

Learner 3: *No, I think it was a jersey.*

5 Finally, show the picture to the class again.

Note

In case the learners find it difficult to talk about the picture, have a number of questions ready.

Variation 1 Picture in groups

Preparation	You will need a picture of a scene containing objects and people for each group of learners.

1 Give each group a picture of a scene including objects and people. They must prepare 10 to 15 questions on this picture.
2 Then ask one learner to show their group's picture to another group for 30 seconds.
3 *Either* ask the two groups to join together and invite the first group to ask their questions, *or* ask each of the learners from the first group to find a partner from the second group, and put their questions to them.

Variation 2 Clothes

Preparation	You will need a collection of clothing and accessories (e.g. sunglasses, gloves) large enough for learners to wear over their normal clothes.

1 Give the collection of clothing and accessories to one learner, and ask them to leave the classroom and put on some of the items.
2 Invite them to come into the classroom for a few seconds before going out again.
3 Ask the class to try to describe what their classmate was wearing.

Variation 3 A mini drama

Preparation	Arrange for a smash-and-grab raid in the classroom! Before the lesson starts, explain your plan to two learners. Tell them to dress up in strange clothes, enter the classroom, seize a variety of objects, putting some into a bag, others into their pockets, and carrying the remainder. They should then leave the classroom. The whole 'raid' should not take more than a few seconds. Alert the 'thieves' to the fact that everyone needs to be able to see what they are doing. So, they should not turn their backs on the class, for example.

1 Stand back in mock helplessness as the 'raid' takes place.
2 Once the 'raid' is over, ask the class to describe the appearance and actions of the 'thieves', and to tell you which objects were 'stolen'.

7.21 Kim's memory game (Variations 6 and 7)

See 6.12 Kim's memory game for the main game and Variations 1 to 5.

Variation 6 Present perfect, past simple, prepositions

Language	Detecting and describing changes in position orally using the present perfect (e.g. *You've put ...*), past simple (e.g. *It was ...*), and prepositions (e.g. *next to ...*)
Preparation	You will need a collection of objects, as in the main game. (See also step 1 below.)

1 Place six to eight objects on a table. Make sure that several of them are positioned, for example, on top of, underneath, next to, and/or inside other objects.
2 After 20 seconds, ask the learners to look away. Change the position of one of the objects.

Teacher: *What have I done?*
Learner: *You've put the tape underneath the dictionary.*
Teacher: *And where was it?*
Learner: *It was next to the watch.*

Variation 7 Present perfect and comparisons

Language	Detecting changes made to a drawing and describing them orally using the present perfect and comparatives (e.g. *You've made the tree taller.*)

1 Instead of using objects or prepared pictures, as in the main game, ask a number of learners to draw some simple objects on the board. Some of the objects might have colour on them.
2 Tell the learners to close their eyes whilst you, or a learner, *change* some of the drawings, making them longer or shorter, fatter, taller, greener, etc.

3 Challenge the class to tell you what you have done. For example:

Teacher: *What have I done?*
Learner: *You've made the tree taller.*

or:

Teacher: *What is different?*
Learner: *The tree is taller.*

Note

The learners can play the same game in pairs using paper, pencil and rubber.

CREATE

7.22 Alibis

| Family | CREATE |
| Language | Collaboratively making up an alibi accounting for one's location, actions and motivations for a three-hour period of time, and attempting to memorise all the details
Independently narrating invented past events and answering questions about them as accurately as possible, using the past simple in both cases
Asking questions about past events, using the past simple |

Procedure

1 Invite learners to work in pairs, imagining that they have to create an alibi for a given evening. Tell them they must produce a story that accounts for every minute between 7 p.m. and 10 p.m. during the evening, then try to memorise all the information they have invented.
2 When the learners have prepared their alibis, tell one pair that they are now being called into the police station for questioning. Ask one of the two 'suspects' to wait outside while the other faces the rest of the class. Encourage the class to question the first 'suspect' at length to find out the details of the alibi.
3 Invite the second 'suspect' in, and let the class subject him or her to a similar interrogation, attempting to find inconsistencies in the 'stories' and looking for contradictions between them. If they find any, the alibi is broken and the class wins. If not, the two who made up the alibi win.

> **Examples of questions that the class might prepare, and then use when interrogating the 'suspects'**
> *Where were you at 7.15 p.m?*
> *Who else was there?*
> *What time did you leave?*
> *What did you do next?*
> *Why did you go there?*
> *Did you speak to anyone?*
> *How much did it cost?*
> *Who paid?*
> *Did you get any change?*
> *When did you leave?*
> *How did you get home?*

Note

An alternative procedure is to divide the class into two interviewing teams. Each team takes it in turn to interview each learner. A time limit is given, for example, five minutes. The first team to note an inconsistency wins. If neither team notes an inconsistency between the statements of the two 'accused' then they are proclaimed innocent and free to go!

7.23 Passing on a story

Family	CREATE
Language	Making up stories collectively, using the past simple and past continuous as well as a wide range of language points

Procedure

1 Explain to the learners that you are going to begin a story and that they must continue it, each learner in turn adding a sentence or part of a sentence. Make sure to include a verb in the past tense in your starting phrase or sentence, so the learners will continue the story in the past. You can contribute to the story periodically if you feel it would help to give it a boost.

2   Retell the story with each learner contributing his or her sentence, in
    sequence.

Teacher:	*I saw a horse sitting ...*
Learner 1:	*... in the kitchen.*
Teacher:	*It was eating ...*
Learner 2:	*... a piece of cake ...*
Learner 3:	*... and drinking tea from a bucket.*
Teacher:	*I said ...*
Learner 4:	*'Don't you have milk in your tea?'*

3   When the story is finished, ask the learners to write their version of it.

Variation 1   Remembering and continuing a story

Follow the same game procedure as above, only in this variation ask each
learner to remember and repeat all the previous contributions! This should
not be seen as a test! Learners may help a classmate who is stuck.

Some examples of sentences you might begin the story with

In the middle of last night I was lying in bed when I heard a strange noise ...
Last Saturday I went to the shops and I saw ...
I opened the door and there was ...
The woman was crying, and she said ...
I heard the wolves howling ...

7.24   Interrupting a story

Family	CREATE
Language	Asking questions, using present, past or future tenses according to
	the tense forms the storyteller uses

Procedure

Try to tell a story or describe an experience in less than five minutes.
Challenge the learners to prevent you from doing so by interrupting you with
questions about the story (any questions!) which you must stop your
storytelling to answer.

Teacher:	*There was a man who ...*
Learner 1:	*What was his name?*
Teacher:	*Henry.*
Learner 2:	*What was his family name?*
Teacher:	*Ponsonberry.*
Learner 3:	*What did he eat for breakfast?*
etc.	

Note

You might like to divide the class into two teams and give them one point for every question asked.

7.25 Pattern poems

Family	CREATE
Language	Using the present simple for everyday activities (e.g. *I get up at seven o'clock*), and contrasting them with activities in progress, using the present continuous (e.g. *I am lying in bed*), following a model provided to channel the poet's creativity
	Focussing on almost any language point through the writing of poetry
Preparation	The poetry-writing activity presented here requires almost no preparation. You need only choose a 'frame' in which poems can be created, and concentrate on the intended language focus. Possible 'frames' are presented below.

Procedure

1 Help the learners to brainstorm a few sentences, using the present simple tense, about their everyday lives. Write these sentences on the board.

2 Ask the learners to write five more sentences of their own.

3 Invite the learners, working in groups of four, to select a total of four of the sentences taken from any of the ones they have written. They should write them in a list under the first line of *Every day*.

4 Next, tell all the groups that they should add a new line, *But now, but now*.

5 Encourage the learners to brainstorm together at least ten sentences containing the present continuous. Their sentences should represent their ideal dream alternatives to their everyday lives!

6 Ask the learners to choose four of their present continuous sentences and list them under *But now, but now*.
7 Invite the learners to compose a line to finish off their poem.
8 Finally, ask each group to find a dramatic way of performing their poem for the class.

Every day,
I get up at seven o' clock.
I get dressed.
I eat my breakfast.
I go to school.

But now, but now,
I am lying in bed.
I am listening to some music.
I am eating chocolate.
And I am thinking of my friends.
It's Sunday.

Sometimes,
I sing and
Run in the mountains and
Swim in the lakes and
Fly and
Dream.

But now, but now,
I'm sitting in school.
I'm not
Singing and running and swimming and flying and
  dreaming.

Possible frames of patterns and tenses as a basis for writing poems based on repetition
Friendship is …
I have always … but in future I will …
I would have liked to … but I didn't.
He can run faster than me … but I can …
If I were a swallow I would fly to …
I wish I had … but I don't …

8 Solo games

Learners benefit from learning and or revising aspects of language during private study time or for homework. The games in this chapter will help them with this sort of study. Some of the solo games also lend themselves to follow-up with a partner. The games here are a small selection only; other activities suitable for solo use can be found elsewhere in the book.

We suggest that, if possible, you prepare the learners for any intended solo games by trying them out in class beforehand, under your direction. In this way, the learners will feel clear and confident about using the games without your direct support.

It is helpful to give the learners an opportunity to experience how to select and apply different types of game to suit their specific needs. It is our aim to promote 'learning how to learn', with something suitable for different learning styles.

We suggest that you help your learners to recognise their preferred ways of learning by giving copies of pages 172 and 173 to them and then going through the list discussing each style. To show that we all make use of all the styles, you might like to ask the learners to put the styles into their order of importance for them as individuals.

For the learners' convenience, and yours, Cambridge University Press are happy to give you permission to photocopy the pages in this chapter marked **PHOTOCOPIABLE** for the learners to keep.

You have got 1000 million brain cells!
More than the number of stars in the galaxy!
Here is how to use them

You are amazing!

You have an amazing memory! You can remember thousands of people and places. You can remember many techniques to do with your mobile phone and your computer. You have remembered at least 10,000 words in your own language. No problem! You have an amazing memory!

******

There are many ways to learn

We all learn in different ways: **looking, listening, moving, being crazy, creating, being serious.**
Use all these ways and find your own favourite way of learning …
but still **use all the ways**.

******

Do you like to *look* at things?

Write down the words you want to learn.
Put pictures with each word.
Choose or draw crazy pictures if you can.
Make diagrams explaining the words.
Use different colours.

******

Do you like to *listen* to things?

Say the words you want to learn aloud.
Exaggerate the rhythm of the words.
Dramatise the words; say them aloud with feeling.
Write the words so that you can see how they sound.
Play music in the background while you learn.

******

Do you like to *move* about and *touch* things?

Make word and picture cards and move them around.
Beat the rhythm of the words with your finger.
Walk about when you learn words.
Use real objects when you can.
Mime the different words.

Do you like to *be crazy*?
Make up crazy pictures to illustrate words you want to learn.
Make up crazy sentences to go with pictures.
Laugh and learn.

* * * * * * * *

Do you like to *create* things?
Put words together which sound nearly the same and are
funny together,
for example, *fat cat, turkey in Turkey, a horse of course.*
Write poems with the words.
Invent as many different conversations as possible.
Write a letter, a story, a joke or words for a song.

* * * * * * * *

Do you like to *think* seriously?
Find your own ways of learning.
Find ways of explaining points of grammar.
Find ways of grouping and ordering words.
List all the words you can think of which you associate with a topic.
Make up as many sentences as you can about the topic.
Explain your ideas to other people.

* * * * * * * *

Do *things* with the language
Use your brain *to do* things with the language. Just looking and
reading will not help you enough.

* * * * * * * *

Work! Break! Work! Break! *Work! Break!* Work! Break! Work! Break!
Work for 10 to 15 minutes and then stop. Do something else for
5 minutes: listen to music; jump up and down (this puts oxygen
into your brain). Then work on the same language for another
10 to 15 minutes but with another technique. Make sure you
work on the language you have learned after a few days and then
after a few weeks.

* * * * * * * *

*SOCCER PLAYERS IN TRAINING RUN WITH THE BALL BETWEEN
STICKS SO THEY CAN **PLAY** SOCCER BETTER!
SINGERS SING DOH – RAY – ME SO THEY CAN **SING** BETTER!
YOU CAN PLAY THESE GAMES AND BOOST YOUR LANGUAGE POWER*

8.1 Folding vocabulary book

To learn and revise words

1   Many people have a vocabulary book. The mother-tongue words are written down one side and the English words are on the other side. It may be difficult to learn words like that.

2   Try folding the page down the middle and keeping half the page folded back and hidden. Then you can really test yourself.

3   Go for your own record! How fast can you get all the words right? Every time you make a mistake you must start again. Or …

4   Cut each word in the half page which folds back into a strip. You can fold each word strip back or bring it forwards again.

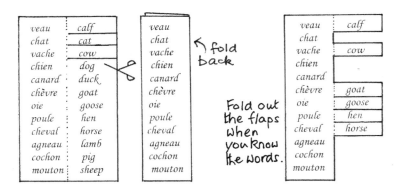

Note

When you learn words in a list, you learn best the words at the beginning and end of the list. You often forget the words in the middle. Write the list again and put the middle words at the top or bottom of your new list.

8.2 Cards

To learn and revise words, sentences or grammar

1 Write the English word (or sentence, or bit of grammar) on one side of the card and your own language word on the other side.
2 Put all the cards with your language side up. Turn them over, learning the English words. Put them back again with your language side up.
3 When you think you know them all, test and time yourself. Start again each time you make a mistake.

Note

There are lots of things you can put on cards, for example:

- Write an English sentence on one side and draw a picture to illustrate it on the other.
- Write a word on one side, and on the other side write one or two sentences which contain the word.
- Write an English sentence on one side and the same sentence, in your language, on the other.
- Write a question on one side and the answer on the other.
- Write an English word on one side and the English dictionary definition of it on the other.
- Write half a word on one side and the other half of the word on the other side (so as to practise spelling).
- Write opposites, e.g. *big / small* on each side of the card.

He has climbed the mountain .

8.2 Cards (*continued*)

Some advice
1 Use cards about 2 cm x 5 cm.
2 Use colour to make the words and the pictures special.
3 Try to make the pictures a bit crazy. You will remember them better.
4 *Apple* is easy to draw. Try using a symbol for abstract words, for example, *love*. You might have to invent the symbol or use a cartoon symbol for example, a light bulb over somebody's head means 'an idea'.

8.3 Match the cards

To learn and revise words or sentences

1 Write the English word (or sentence, or bit of grammar, etc.) on one card. On a second card draw a picture to illustrate it. (Or see **8.2 Cards** for more ideas on what to put on the cards. Note that for this game you only write/draw on one side of each card.)

2 Mix all the cards face up on the table. Then put them together in pairs. Time how long it takes.

3 Now put all the cards face down. Mix them up on the table.

4 Try to remember what each card is and try to remember where each pair is. Turn two cards over and see if you can make a pair. If not, turn them face down and try again. Time how long it takes you to put all the cards into pairs.

5 Later, you could challenge a friend to play this game with you. First, challenge them to beat your record with the cards face up. Then turn the cards face down and see who can win the most pairs.

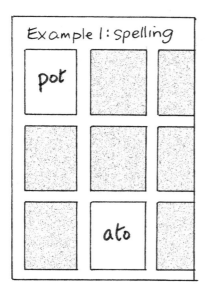
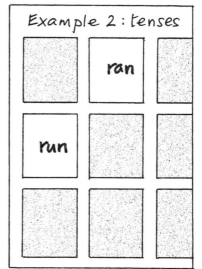

Example 1: Spelling

pot

ato

Example 2: tenses

ran

run

8.4 **Match the halves**

To revise the spelling of a list of words, for example *apple, banana, bean, cabbage, chicken, chips, milk, potato.*

1   First write out the list of words you must learn. Then make a second list of the *beginning* of each word and a third list showing the *end* of each word. The endings in the third list must be in a different order from the beginnings.

apple	ap	ato
banana	ban	bage
bean	be	ken
cabbage	cab	ple
chicken	chic	lk
chips	ch	ana
milk	mi	an
potato	pot	ips

2   Cover up your list of complete words. Look at the other two lists and try to write all the words in full. Say the words to yourself as you write them.

3   Compare your new list with the original list to make sure that your words are correct.

Note

You can do this activity alone or with a partner.

8.5 Word snakes

To help you to remember sentences

1   Copy the sentences, but don't leave spaces between the words. For example:
He let the cat out of the bag. (= He accidentally told someone a secret.)

Heletthecatoutofthebag.

I'msorrycouldyousaythatagainplease?

2   Do something else for ten minutes, for example, listen to some music.
3   Look at your 'word snakes' again and write them out, leaving the correct spaces between the words. Say the sentences to yourself as you write them.

8.6 Odd-one-out

To revise words you know or should know

1 Write words in groups of four. In each group, include an 'odd-one-out' – a word which is different from the others. Look at the example:

    boots   **shoes**   **sandals**   **hat**

The odd-one-out is *hat*, because you wear it on your head, but you wear all the others on your feet.

2 Show your groups of words to a partner. Ask your partner to tell you the odd-one-out in each group and to explain why. Do you agree?

3 Later try to show that each word in a group can be the odd-one-out. For example: *sandals*, might be the odd-one-out because you can only wear them in hot weather.

8.7 Different groups of words

To revise words from different topics

Example of words from different topics

shopping	cinema	wool	basket	language
maths	job	magazine	chicken	dinner
exam	cotton	sweater	trousers	money
friends				

---

1 Organise the words into at least four groups. It is not necessary for each group to have the same number of words. Words can go in more than one group. Write your groups of words.

2 Later, it may be interesting to compare your grouping of words with a partner's grouping. Can you understand the logic of your partner's groups? Can you explain the logic of your groups?

Example of different groups

FOOD	STUDY AND WORK	CLOTHES	FREE TIME
shopping	language	sweater	cinema
dinner	maths	trousers	magazine
chicken	exam	wool	friends
basket	job	cotton	money
money	money	money	

Note

If you write the words on cards, it makes it easier to move them around into different groups.

8.8 Mind map

To revise sets of words or phrases relating to a topic

In mind maps the ideas spread all over the page. You can connect
ideas and group them. You can colour them and make the lines thick
or thin and the bubbles big or small depending on how important the
ideas are to you and what you feel about them.

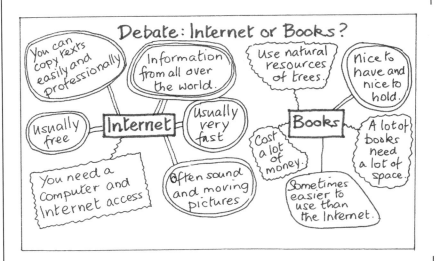

Examples of sets of words or grammatical points for mind maps
Story: ideas, words and phrases you need for your story
Person: describing a person in different ways
Debate: different ways of looking at a topic
Exams: the information you must learn
Pronunciation: spelling and sound (Example: 'ough' words (enough/rough)
(cough) (through) (thought/bought/caught) (bough/bow/cow)
(though/sew)

8.9 Word Sun

To learn or revise a set of words or phrases relating to a topic.

1   Draw a circle and write the topic word in capital letters in the middle, for example: FRUIT
2   Then write other related words around your circle to make a Word Sun.

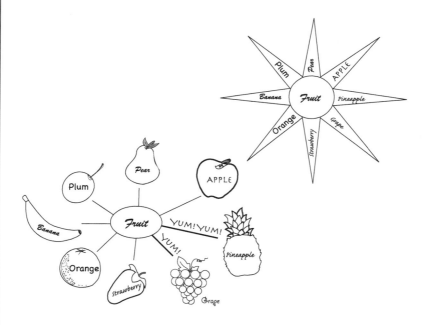

Use pictures and colour to help you remember. For example, draw little pictures of each fruit and write the words on the fruit. Use a colour or the thickness of your line to show how often you eat each fruit or how much you like the fruit.

3   Give yourself three seconds to 'photograph' this in your mind.
4   Cover your Word Sun and try to make an *exact* copy of it.
5   Compare your copy with the original. If they are not identical, try again until you write a perfect copy.

8.10 Steps

To revise words which are related
Arrange the words like stairs or a ladder, showing gradual changes of
meaning, step by step.

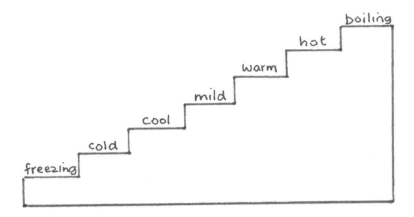

Other examples of revising words with steps
absolutely impossible, impossible, very difficult, difficult, fairly difficult,
not difficult, easy, very easy
none, a few, several, quite a few, quite a lot, a lot, many,
hundreds/thousands, countless
tiny, small, average-sized, big, large, enormous, gigantic

8.11 Add a word

To revise a set of words on a topic (for example, shopping, food, home life)

1 Write any word, then add a word which this first word makes you think of. Join the two words with a line.
2 Continue adding words as you think of them, making a chain of meaning.

drink — water — cold — hot — tea — eat
bread — butter — cheese — sandwich — food
kitchen — cook — oven

3 Later show your connections to a partner. Try to guess why your partner has made his or her connections.

8.12 Add a sentence

To practise writing about a topic (for example, home life, holidays, shopping, advertising)

1 Choose a topic and write a sentence connected with the topic.
2 Then add a sentence which is in some way connected to the first sentence.
3 Continue the 'chain' of sentences for as long as possible.

Example
I like my room.
It's small.
My name is on the door.
There are lots of posters on the wall.
I've got a computer.

8.13 Favourites

To revise a set of words (for example, words for jobs, food, clothes, sports)

It helps you to learn words if you write them out in a way which is important for *you*.

1   Write lists of things, starting with the one you like *most* and ending with the one you like *least*. Write the words you like most in big letters and the words you like least in very small letters.

Examples of sets of words you can put in a list
colours
sports
jobs
food
musical instruments

---

2   Later, work with a partner. Write the words in the order you think your partner has written them.
3   Compare your lists and see how well you know each other!

Fat French fries
Fruit cake
Sausages
Baked potatoes
Pancakes
Burgers
Thin French fries
Snails

8.14 Lose the vowels

To revise the spelling of a list of words

1 Write the words, omitting all the vowels (the letters a, e, i, o and u), for example:

teacher	→	tchr
word	→	wrd
learn	→	lrn

2 Look at your list of words without vowels and try to write out all the words in full. Say each word to yourself a few times as you write it.

3 Compare your new list with the original to make sure that all your words are correct. You can time yourself. Do it again and see if you can do it faster.

4 Later, look at the list of words without vowels and see if you can still remember the complete words.

5 Later, show your list of words without vowels to a friend and see if he or she can work out what the words are.

Variation 1 Remember the vowels

Write the words, putting a dash instead of the vowels (the letters a, e, i, o and u), for example:

geography	→	g _ _ gr_ phy
English	→	_ ngl_ sh
history	→	h_ st_ ry
music	→	m_ s_ c

8.15 Write a crazy story

To help you to revise and remember words

1   Put all the words you must remember into a story ... make it a
crazy story and then you will remember the story and the words.
For example:

Where are my teeth?

The lion said, 'Where are my teeth?'

He looked in the hippo's mouth. 'Are they **in** the hippo's
mouth?'

He looked behind the dinosaur. 'Are they **behind** the
dinosaur?'

He looked under the alligator. 'Are they **under** the alligator?'

He looked behind the hippo. 'Are they **behind** the hippo?'

He found them in his pocket! 'No! They are **in** my pocket!'

2   Later, tell your story to other learners.

8.16 Write a dramatic dialogue

To remember grammar

1 Write a mini dialogue including the grammatical point you want
   to remember, for example, ... *is so* ... *that*. Make it funny or
   dramatic!

> A: *My father is so strong he can lift a lawnmower with one
>   hand.*
>
> B: *Huh, that's nothing! My father is so strong he can lift two
>   lawnmowers with one hand.*
>
> A: *Huh, that's nothing! My father is so strong he can lift a
>   garden shed above his head.*
>
> B: *Huh, that's nothing! My father is so strong he can throw a
>   garden shed a hundred metres.*

2 Later, act out your dialogue for other learners.

8.17 Be dramatic

To remember words and phrases

1 Try saying ordinary words and phrases in a dramatic way.
   For example, you are in the desert and you have no food. You are
   thinking of all the food you know. You say each word for food,
   dramatically, desperately ...
   'Sandwiches, tomato sauce, bread, ...'

2 Later, act this out for other learners.

Sssssandwiches!

8.18 Make a crossword

To learn or revise a list of words, for example, *music, theatre, football, swimming, tennis, play, like, concert, listen, disco, chess, hockey, hate.*

If you use a dictionary you can learn the meanings of new words as well as revise old ones.

1   Write the words in a crossword grid.

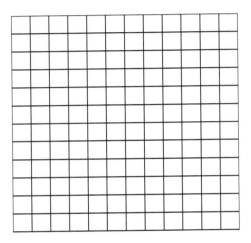

2   Write clues for your crossword, for example:
    Across
    1 You go to a concert to listen to ....
    Down
    3 I go .... in the river.

3   Later, exchange your crossword and clues with a partner and see if you can do each other's crossword.

Index

Index

Made in the USA
San Bernardino, CA
11 December 2012